Popular Canadian Curriculum Se

MW01677486

Canadian Curriculum SummerSmart®

3·4

Credits

Photos (Front Cover "children" Gennadiy Poznyakov/123RF.com, "beach toys" serezniy/123RF.com, "beach" Alexandr Ozerov/123RF.com. Back Cover "children" Anatoliy Samara/123RF.com, "school bus" Thomas Bedenk/123RF.com, "children" Dmitriy Shironosov/123RF.com, "classroom" Franck Boston/123RF.com, "girl looking at grass" Sergiy Bykhunenko/123RF.com, "girl blowing windmill" Logos/123RF.com, "bee" szefei/123RF.com, "lorikeets" Tyler Panian/123RF.com, "children" Anatoliy Samara/123RF.com, "Chateau Frontenac" Susan Peterson/123RF.com)

Printed in China

ISBN: 978-1-77149-145-7

Contents

Grades 3–4

Week

ISBN: 978-1-77149-145-7

Week

ISBN: 978-1-77149-145-7

Dear Parent:

While all work and no play makes Jack a dull boy, all play and no work would probably make Jack forget most of what he has learned, which is why it is necessary to schedule regular practice in the long summer vacation to help your child consolidate what he or she has learned.

This is where Canadian Curriculum SummerSmart can help.

Canadian Curriculum SummerSmart provides practice for your child to review the essentials taught in the previous academic year and prepares him or her for the grade ahead with confidence. The series is organized in an easy-to-use format: each title is made up of eight weeks (units) of work so your child can complete one unit each week during the summer vacation. The units are comprised of practice in English, Math, Science, and Social Studies. Engaging Arts and Crafts activities, as well as Comics and Fun Places to Go in Summer, are also included for added fun.

Your child will be delighted to have Canadian Curriculum SummerSmart as his or her summer learning buddy.

Your Partner in Education,
Popular Book Company (Canada) Limited

ISBN: 978-1-77149-145-7

Week 1

English

- read a passage and put events in order
- add adjectives to sentences
- create new sentences with given words
- make compound words

Mathematics

- understand and complete number patterns
- solve word problems
- read and interpret graphs
- understand fractions and complete the drawings

Science

- identify producers and consumers
- complete food chains

Social Studies

- learn about the feudal system of medieval Europe
- learn about the caste system of medieval India

ISBN: 978-1-77149-145-7

A. Read the story.

Marco the Magician

Marco loves magic. He used all sorts of books and props to learn how to perform magic tricks. His family suggested that he put on a show for his friends and neighbours. Marco thought this was a great idea.

Marco's sister, Rosa, made beautiful, bright signs that she posted all around the neighbourhood. Marco's dad helped him set up the backyard. Together, they built a small stage and used old sheets for curtains. Marco's mom decided to make chocolate chip cookies and pink lemonade to serve the audience.

On the day of the show, the backyard was packed. Rosa acted as Marco's assistant. She welcomed the guests and announced, "Ladies and gentlemen, boys and girls, I now present to you Marco the Magician!" The crowd applauded loudly as Marco burst through the curtains onto the stage. He entertained the audience with card tricks and some of his jokes. He waved his magic wand and "PRESTO", he pulled a white rabbit out of his hat. Marco even made Rosa disappear and then with one simple "ABRACADABRA", she was back!

After the show, the audience enjoyed the delicious refreshments prepared by Marco's mom. As they left, they congratulated Marco and told him they would be back for his next show.

ISBN: 978-1-77149-145-7

B. Read the paragraph that summarizes the story. Put a line through the sentence that does not belong.

Marco loves magic. He learned magic tricks by reading books and practising. A magician usually wears a top hat. Marco decided to put on a show for his neighbours and friends. His family helped with the preparations. Marco put on a spectacular performance and everyone loved his show.

C. Help Marco complete a schedule for his magic show. Number the events to put them in order.

Magic Show
Schedule

◯ Do card tricks.

◯ Pull a rabbit from my hat.

◯ Rosa welcomes the guests.

◯ Make Rosa disappear and then reappear.

◯ Serve mother's cookies and lemonade to the guests.

ISBN: 978-1-77149-145-7

D. Add an adjective to describe each underlined noun. Write a complete sentence.

1. A <u>magician</u> can fool the audience.

____

____

2. Marco put on a <u>performance</u>.

____

____

3. A <u>rabbit</u> came out of Marco's <u>hat</u>.

____

4. The <u>neighbours</u> gathered in the backyard.

____

5. Rosa hung a <u>sign</u> on the fence.

____

6. The <u>lemonade</u> and the <u>cookies</u> were delicious.

____

Week 1

English

ISBN: 978-1-77149-145-7

E. Write a complete sentence using each of the following words.

invisible ______________________________

surprised ______________________________

impossible ______________________________

magician ______________________________

F. Draw lines to match the words to make compound words.

- house
- fly
- room
- book
- glass

ISBN: 978-1-77149-145-7

Week 1

Mathematics

A. The children are collecting cans for their school. Read what they say and fill in the information. Then answer the question.

I've collected 79 cans. I'll collect 1 more can each day.

Day 1: 79
Day 2: ____
Day 3: ____
Day 4: ____
Day 5: ____
Day 6: ____

I've collected 90 cans. I'll collect 2 more cans each day.

Day 1: 90
Day 2: ____
Day 3: ____
Day 4: ____
Day 5: ____
Day 6: ____

I've collected 80 cans. I'll collect 5 more cans each day.

Day 1: 80
Day 2: ____
Day 3: ____
Day 4: ____
Day 5: ____
Day 6: ____

I've collected 25 cans. I'll collect 25 more cans each day.

Day 1: 25
Day 2: ____
Day 3: ____
Day 4: ____
Day 5: ____
Day 6: ____

Who will have collected the most cans after 6 days? ____________

ISBN: 978-1-77149-145-7

B. Help the children solve the problems.

1. Lucy has 427 cans. If she wants to have 500 cans, how many more cans does she need?

   ________ more cans

2. Peter collected 273 cans in May and 185 cans in June. How many cans did Peter collect in all?

   ________ cans

3. If Sue collects 25 more cans, she will have 400 cans in all. How many cans has Sue collected?

   ________ cans

4. This year, Mary collected 98 more cans than she did last year. How many cans did she collect this year?

   ________ cans

ISBN: 978-1-77149-145-7

C. The circle graph shows how many cans were collected by each group in Mrs. Philips's class. Read the graph and answer the questions.

Number of Cans Collected by Each Group

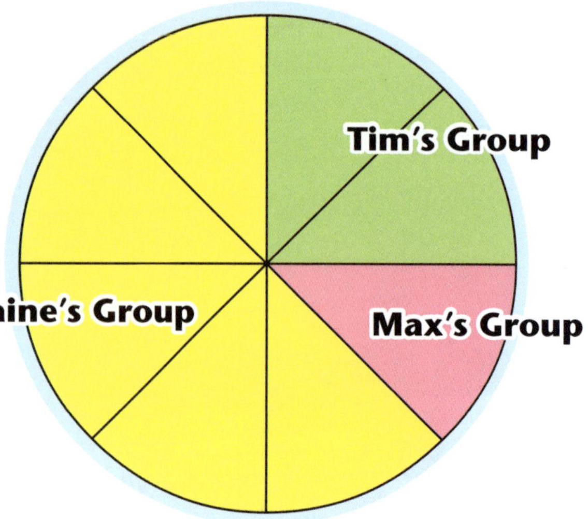

Check the bar graph that correctly shows the information on the circle graph.

1. Which group collected

   a. the most cans? __________

   b. the fewest cans? __________

2. If Max's group collected 100 cans, how many cans did

   a. Tim's group collect?

   __________ cans

   b. Elaine's group collect?

   __________ cans

3.

(A)

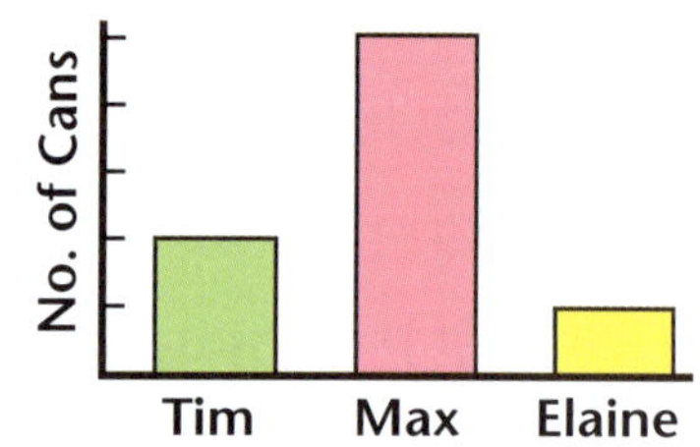

(B)

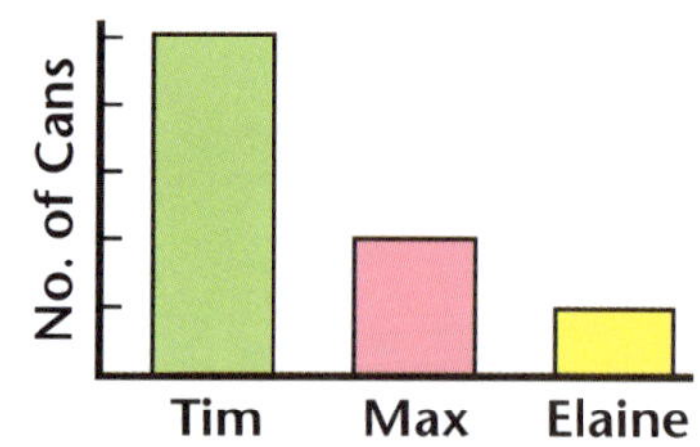

(C)

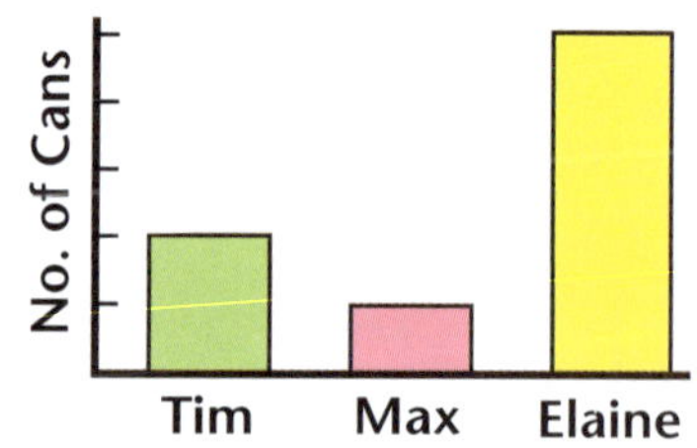

ISBN: 978-1-77149-145-7

D. Read what the children say. Draw the cans and find the number of cans in each recycling box. Then answer the questions.

$\frac{1}{3}$ of my recycling box holds 5 cans. How many cans fit in the box in all?

$\frac{1}{4}$ of my recycling box holds 3 cans. How many cans fit in the box in all?

1. Judy's Recycling Box

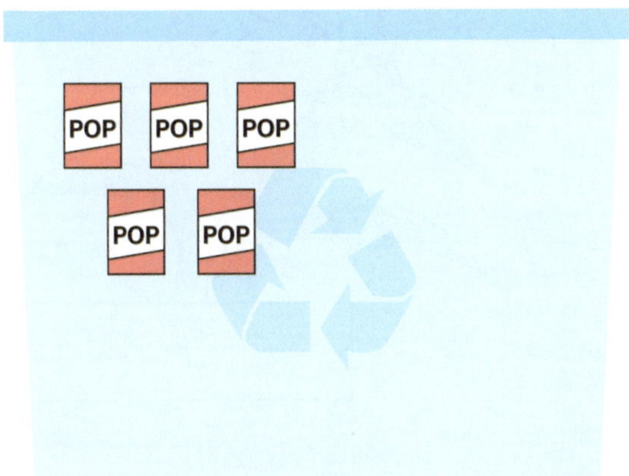

_____ cans in the box

Leon's Recycling Box

_____ cans in the box

2. Whose recycling box holds more cans? _______________

3. If a recycling box can hold up to 200 cans, how many more cans can be put into Judy's box? _______ more cans

ISBN: 978-1-77149-145-7

A. **Label the descriptions as "producers" or "consumers". Then identify each living thing as a "producer" or a "consumer".**

[ ] : organisms that make food using energy from the sun

[ ] : organisms that consume plants or animals

1.

2.

3.

ISBN: 978-1-77149-145-7

B. **What eats what? Trace the arrows and fill in the blanks with the names of the organisms to complete the food chains.**

1.

Food Chain: ________ ----> ________ ----> ________ ----> ________ ----> ________
producer consumer consumer consumer consumer

2. **grasshopper, hawk, snake, clover, frog**

Food Chain: ________ ----> ________ ----> ________ ----> ________ ----> ________
producer consumer consumer consumer consumer

3. **osprey, plankton, water insect, largemouth bass, minnow**

Food Chain: ________ ----> ________ ----> ________ ----> ________ ----> ________
producer consumer consumer consumer consumer

ISBN: 978-1-77149-145-7

A. Fill in the titles of the feudal system. Then circle the correct words to complete the descriptions.

The basic social structure in medieval European society was the feudal system. It had the king at the top with the most power. The peasants were at the bottom of the power structure.

Feudal System

Peasants
Knights

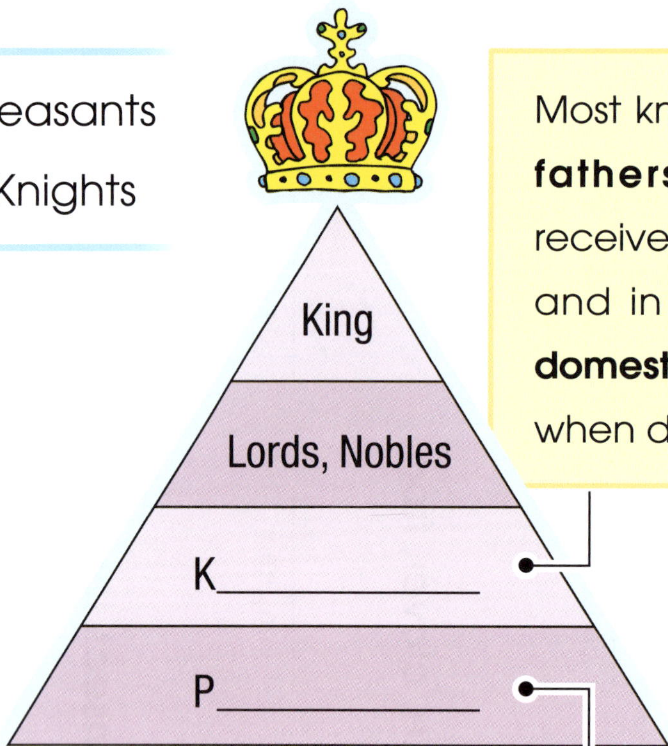

Most knights were the **sons / fathers** of nobles. They received land grants from a lord and in return, they provided **domestic / military** services when demanded by the lord.

Peasants lived in a village surrounding their lord's manor. They worked hard for their lord in exchange for **gifts / protection** and the use of his **land / money**. Most peasants were farmers. They had to pay their lord **rent / money** in the form of goods and labour services.

ISBN: 978-1-77149-145-7

B. Read the passage about the basic social structure in medieval India. Then write the positions of the medieval Indians in the boxes and answer the question.

The Caste System of Medieval India

Much like the feudal system in medieval Europe, the social structure in medieval India also had four levels. The **Brahmins** at the highest level read the sacred texts. Next were the **Kshatriyas**. They were warriors. The **Vaishyas** at the third level were merchants, landowners, and peasants. At the bottom of the caste system were the **Sudras**. Their job was to serve the other three castes.

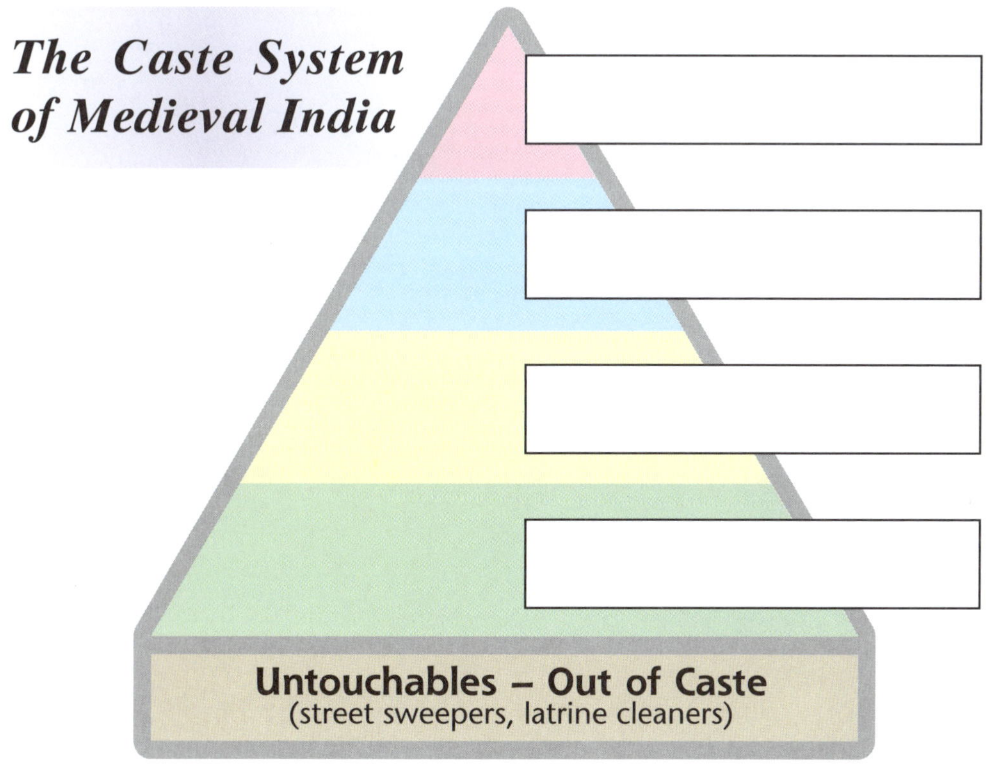

Which group was considered out of caste? What were their duties?

____

ISBN: 978-1-77149-145-7

ISBN: 978-1-77149-145-7

English

- read a passage and fill in the blanks
- put book titles in alphabetical order
- use proper capitalization in book titles
- complete a crossword puzzle

Mathematics

- divide items into groups
- calculate the cost and change for groceries
- complete patterns and measure perimeters
- record temperatures and times

Science

- show the characteristics of animal-pollinated and wind-pollinated flowers
- show different methods of seed dispersal

Social Studies

- identify types of pollution
- complete a table to show past and present farming practices

* The Canadian penny is no longer in circulation. It is used in the unit to show money amounts to the cent.

ISBN: 978-1-77149-145-7

A. Read the passage. Then fill in the blanks.

Mud Puddle, *Love You Forever*, and *The Paper Bag Princess* have one thing in common: they are all books written by the famous author, Robert Munsch.

Robert Munsch was born on June 11, 1945 in Pittsburgh, Pennsylvania. He grew up in a family of nine kids. Munsch, surprisingly, did not do well as a student, but he did write poetry during his years at school. In high school, he did not have many friends, so he spent most of his time reading.

After high school, Robert Munsch studied for seven years to be a priest and worked part-time at an orphanage. It was then that he realized that he was no longer interested in becoming a priest; instead, he enjoyed working with children. He got a job at a daycare. There, he told a story to a group of children. The story was called "Mortimer". Years later, *Mortimer* became a book.

Robert Munsch and his wife then moved to Canada. His boss at a preschool encouraged him to publish his stories. He took two months off and wrote ten stories that he sent to ten publishers. Nine publishers rejected his works but one agreed to publish a story called "Mud Puddle". Since the publication of *Mud Puddle*,

ISBN: 978-1-77149-145-7

Robert Munsch has written more than 50 books. Today, his stories continue to bring smiles to both children and adults all over the world.

1. Robert Munsch is a famous ______________ .
2. He worked part-time at an ______________ .
3. He began telling a story called ______________ to children at a daycare.
4. His first published book was ______________ .

B. Put the books from the Robert Munsch Collection in alphabetical order. Write the titles on the lines.

Mortimer

Stephanie's Ponytail

Angela's Airplane

Andrew's Loose Tooth

The Fire Station

Get Out of Bed

I Have to Go

Millicent and the Wind

Robert Munsch's Books

____

____

____

____

____

____

____

____

ISBN: 978-1-77149-145-7

C. Rewrite each sentence using proper capitalization.

The first word and all the important words in a book's title begin with a capital letter. Sometimes, titles are underlined when they are written.

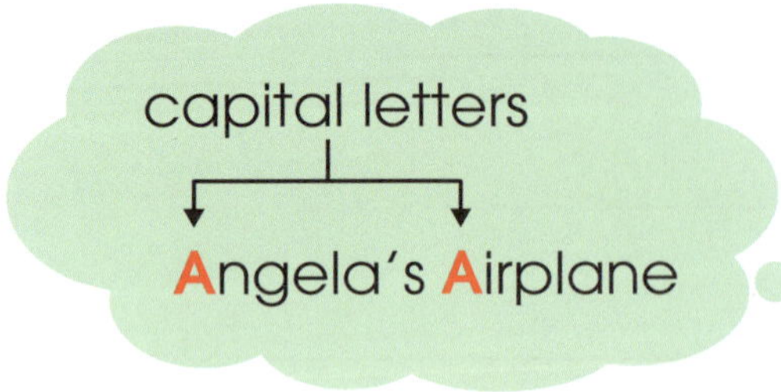

1. mud puddle was Robert Munsch's first published book.

____

2. get out of bed is Peter's favourite book.

____

3. love you forever became a bestseller in Canada.

____

4. the paper bag princess is a book about a brave princess who goes to rescue a prince from a dragon.

____

____

ISBN: 978-1-77149-145-7

D. Read the clues and complete the crossword puzzle with words from the passage.

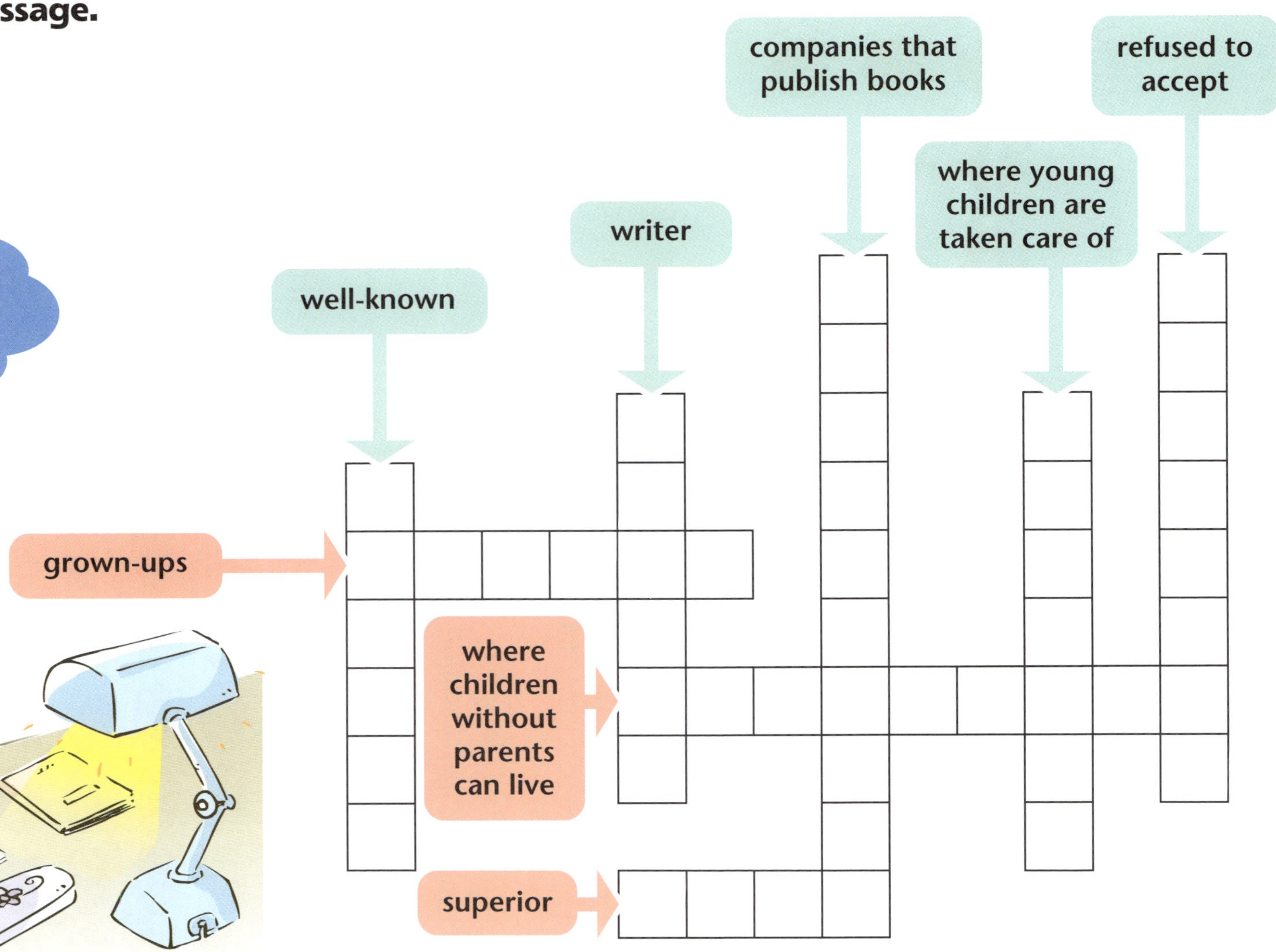

ISBN: 978-1-77149-145-7

Week 2

Mathematics

A. **Help Aunt Daisy organize her groceries. Write the answers on the lines.**

15 cans on 3 shelves

_______ cans on each shelf

12 apples in 2 baskets

_______ apples in each basket

36 cookies on 4 trays

_______ cookies on each tray

20 cans in 5 piles

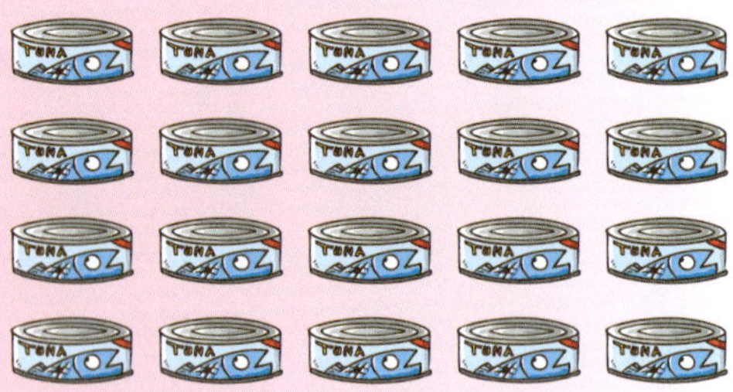

_______ cans in each pile

ISBN: 978-1-77149-145-7

B. Fill out the receipts for Aunt Daisy's purchases.

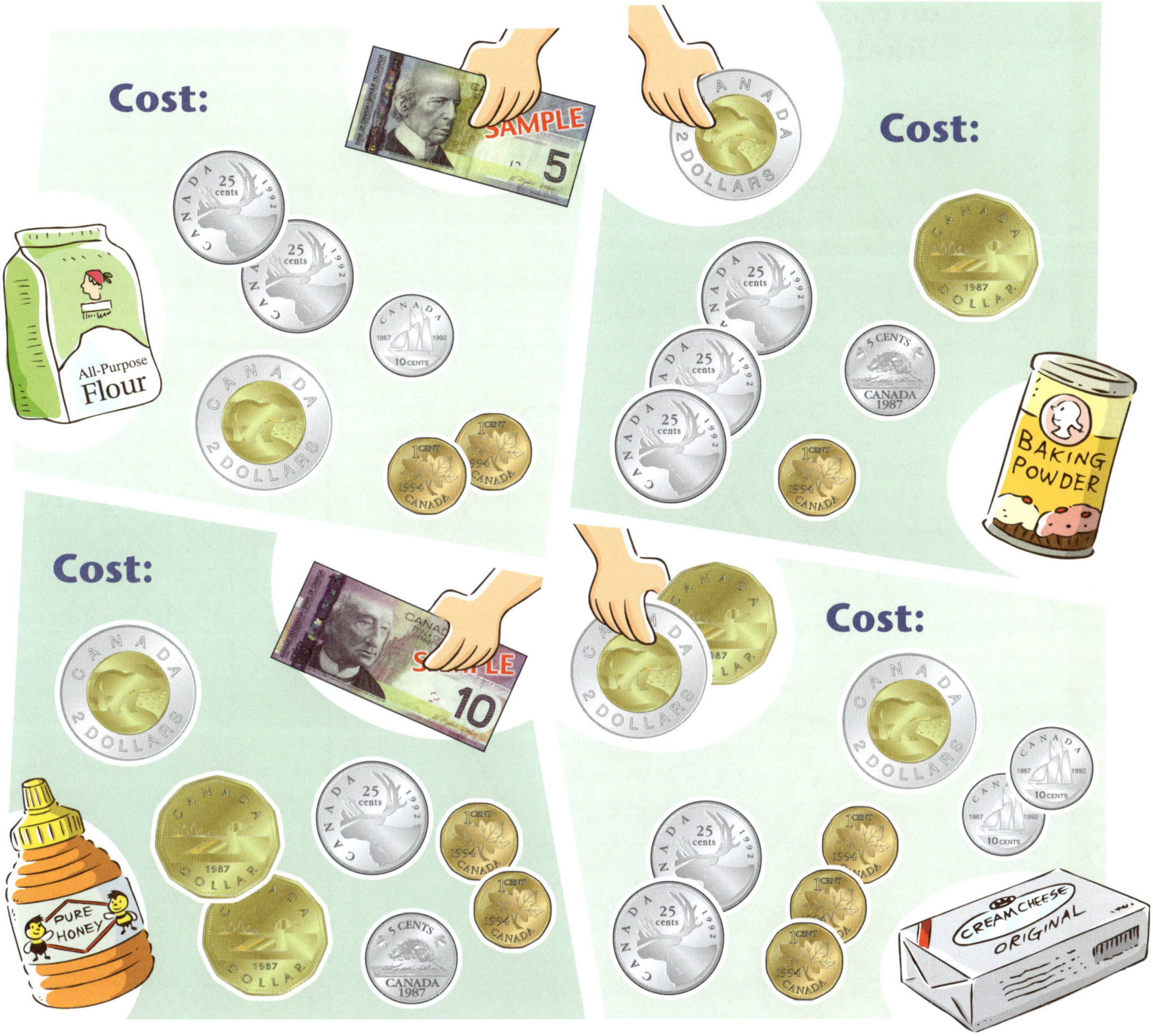

S&M Store

All-Purpose Flour

Cost: $________

Pay: $________

Change:

$________

Hello Mart

Baking Powder

Cost: $________

Pay: $________

Change:

$________

Louis Centre

Honey

Cost: $________

Pay: $________

Change:

$________

Kelly's Grocery

Cream Cheese

Cost: $________

Pay: $________

Change:

$________

ISBN: 978-1-77149-145-7

C. **Aunt Daisy got some raffle tickets. Help her draw the shapes to complete the patterns and do the skill-testing questions on the tickets. Then measure and find the perimeter of each ticket.**

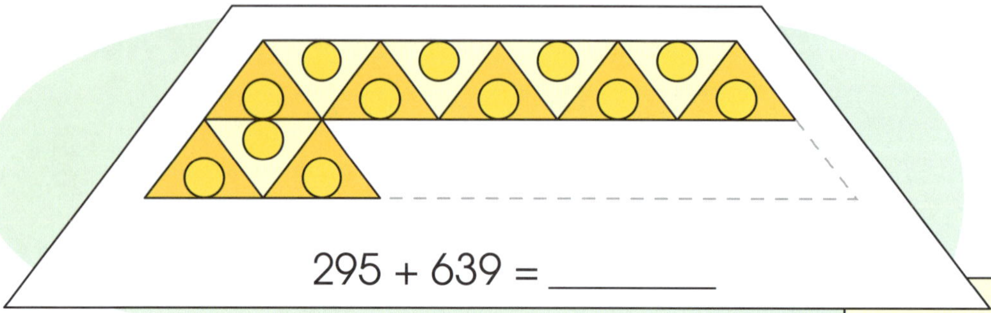

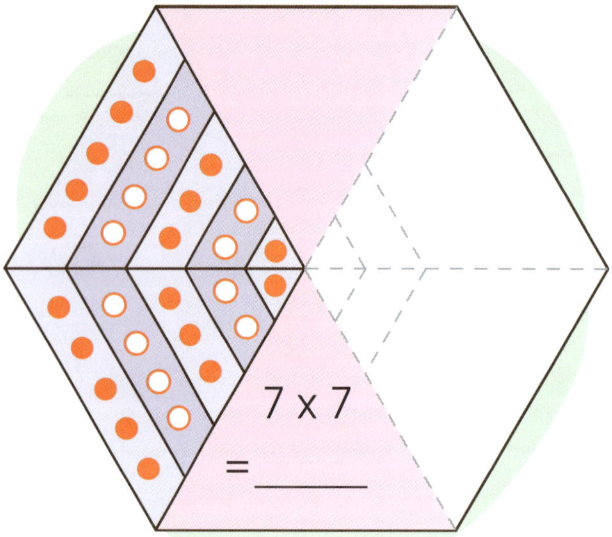

Perimeter

trapezoid ____________

rectangle ____________

hexagon ____________

square ____________

ISBN: 978-1-77149-145-7

D. Help Aunt Daisy record the temperature and the baking time for each food item.

Temperature & Baking Time

_______ °C
_______ min

_______ °C
_______ min

_______ °C
_______ min

_______ °C
_______ min

_______ °C
_______ min

ISBN: 978-1-77149-145-7

Week 2

Science

A. Draw lines to match the characteristics of flowers with the methods of pollination.

Animal Pollination •

Wind Pollination •

- • bright colours
- • sweet nectar
- • usually small
- • light
- • usually big
- • strong scents
- • not attractive

Science Fun

Some plants are pollinated by flies. To attract flies, they smell like rotting meat!

ISBN: 978-1-77149-145-7

B. Match the pictures with the descriptions of seed dispersal methods.

1. eaten by an animal, seeds pass as waste in a different place

2. fall from a plant, "wings" take seeds farther away from the plant

3. hitch a ride on an animal that brushes by the plant

4. buried and forgotten by an animal

5. floats along ocean currents to sprout on a distant shore

ISBN: 978-1-77149-145-7

A. Identify the types of pollution. Then put each type of pollution into the correct part of the diagram.

Types of Pollution (air/water/land/noise)	Causes of Pollution
________ pollution	(A) animal waste dumped on the ground (B) overuse of chemicals on farms
________ pollution	(C) burning wood and coal for fuel
________ pollution	(D) human and farm waste discharged directly into rivers and streams
________ pollution	(E) loud horse-drawn carriages at night

Pollution: Medieval Times and Today

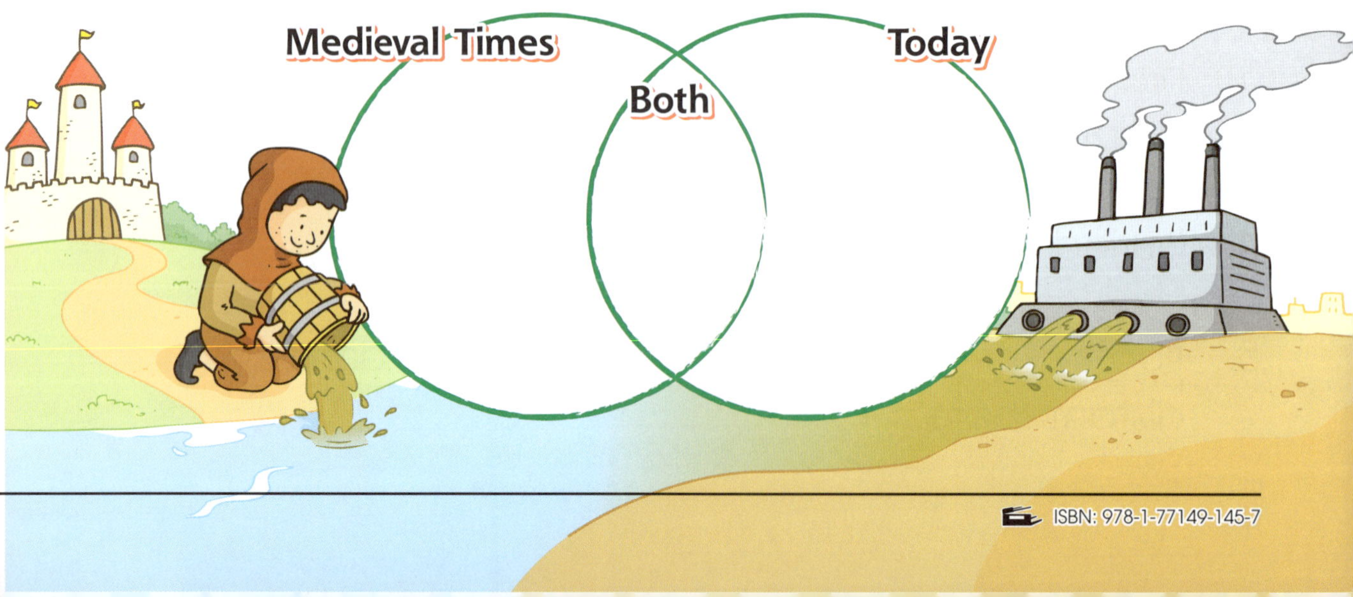

ISBN: 978-1-77149-145-7

B. Farming practices can also cause pollution. Read what the farmers say about their practices in the past and present. Then complete the table.

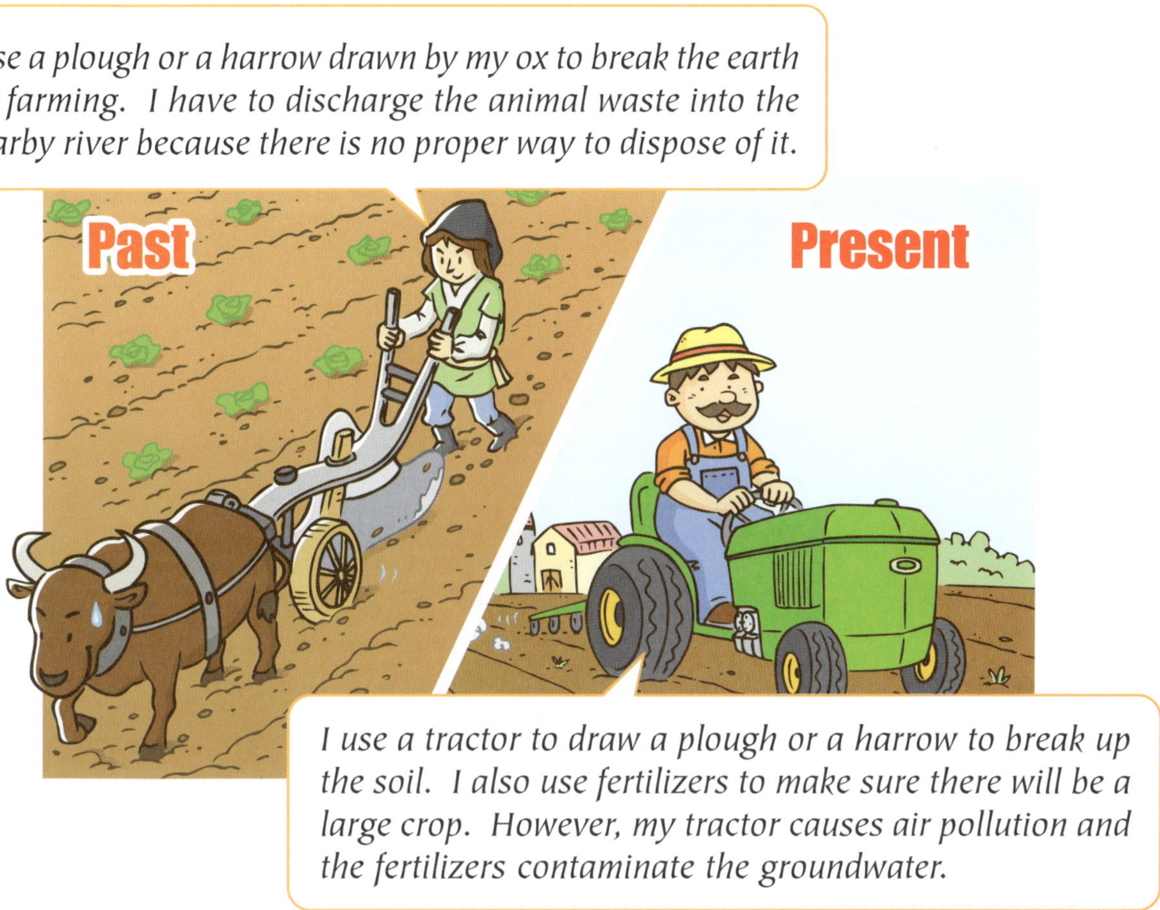

Farming Practices of the Past and Present

Past	Present
Tools used: ____________________	Tools used: ____________________
____________________	____________________
Cause of Pollution:	Cause of Pollution:
____________________	____________________
____________________	____________________

ISBN: 978-1-77149-145-7

ISBN: 978-1-77149-145-7

Week 3

English

- read a passage and answer questions
- rewrite sentences using direct speech
- complete lists
- create a recipe

Mathematics

- divide shapes into equal parts or groups
- find the number of sides and vertices of different shapes, and identify congruent or similar shapes
- answer questions about a pictograph
- draw transformation images

Science

- identify stable and unstable structures
- identify the effects of different forces

Social Studies

- learn about ancient Egyptian and Mesopotamian settlements
- learn about the tools and materials used to build in ancient Egypt

ISBN: 978-1-77149-145-7

A. Read the passage.

A Day with Friends

It was a hot day in August. Julia invited her friends Vanessa and Nadia over for a pool party. While her mom supervised, the girls had swimming races and diving contests, and they even played volleyball in the pool. When they got tired, they floated on air mattresses.

After swimming, Julia's mother invited Vanessa and Nadia to stay for dinner. They had hot dogs, chips, and fresh watermelon. The sun was beginning to set and Julia felt sad that her friends would have to go home soon. Julia's mother said she had a surprise for all of them. She had arranged for Vanessa and Nadia to stay overnight! The girls cheered with delight.

Julia's parents had everything set up in the family room. There were sleeping bags, flashlights, popcorn, and movies for the girls to enjoy. The day was so special that the girls decided to make friendship bracelets for one another. Then they crawled into their sleeping bags and watched a movie as they munched on some popcorn. Later, they told ghost stories and some of their favourite jokes. They giggled and talked for hours. As Julia drifted off to sleep, she thought it was the best day ever.

ISBN: 978-1-77149-145-7

B. Look at the shopping list of Julia's mother. Circle the items that she bought for the party.

Shopping List

movies	*tea*
batteries for flashlights	*candies*
laundry detergent	*popcorn*
noodles	
hot dogs	
gardening gloves	
watermelon	

C. Check the things that you would like to do at a sleepover with your friends. Then write one more idea of your own.

Things to Do at a Sleepover:

- ◯ watch movies
- ◯ play card games
- ◯ tell ghost stories
- ◯ play board games
- ◯ tell jokes
- ◯ bake cookies
- ◯ play sports
- ◯ make friendship bracelets
- ✔ ______________________________

ISBN: 978-1-77149-145-7

D. Write what each person might have said.

Julia invited her friends over for a pool party.

Julia said to her friends, "Would you like to come over for a pool party?"

1. Julia's mother said she had a surprise for all of them.

   ____

   ____

2. Julia asked her mother if they could have pizza for dinner.

   ____

   ____

3. Julia suggested making friendship bracelets for one another.

   ____

   ____

4. Julia told her mother that it was the best day ever.

   ____

   ____

Week 3

English

ISBN: 978-1-77149-145-7

E. Add words to each of the following lists. Use these words to create a recipe for a good friend.

Characteristics of a Good Friend

- kindness
- trust
- patience
- friendliness
- ____________
- ____________
- ____________

Measurements

- cup
- teaspoon
- ____________
- ____________

Recipe Words

- mix
- add
- ____________
- ____________

My Recipe

for Being a Good Friend

1. Add 1 cup of kindness.
2. ______________________________
3. ______________________________
4. ______________________________

ISBN: 978-1-77149-145-7

A. Help the children draw lines to divide the shapes and do the colouring. Then write fractions to complete the sentences.

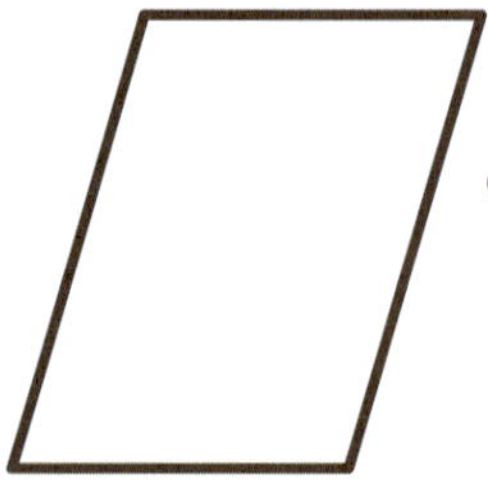

_____ of the shape is coloured.

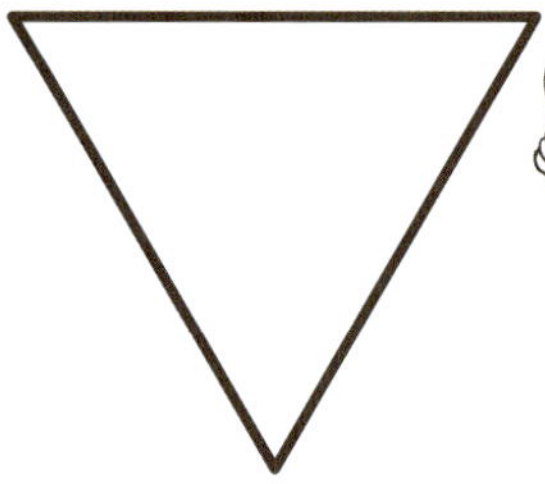

_____ of the shape is coloured.

_____ of the shapes are coloured.

_____ of the shapes are coloured.

ISBN: 978-1-77149-145-7

B. Look at the children's shapes again. Name the shapes and write the number of sides and vertices that each shape has.

_______ sides _______ _______ _______

_______ vertices _______ _______ _______

C. Identify the shapes. Colour the ones that are congruent or similar to the coloured ones.

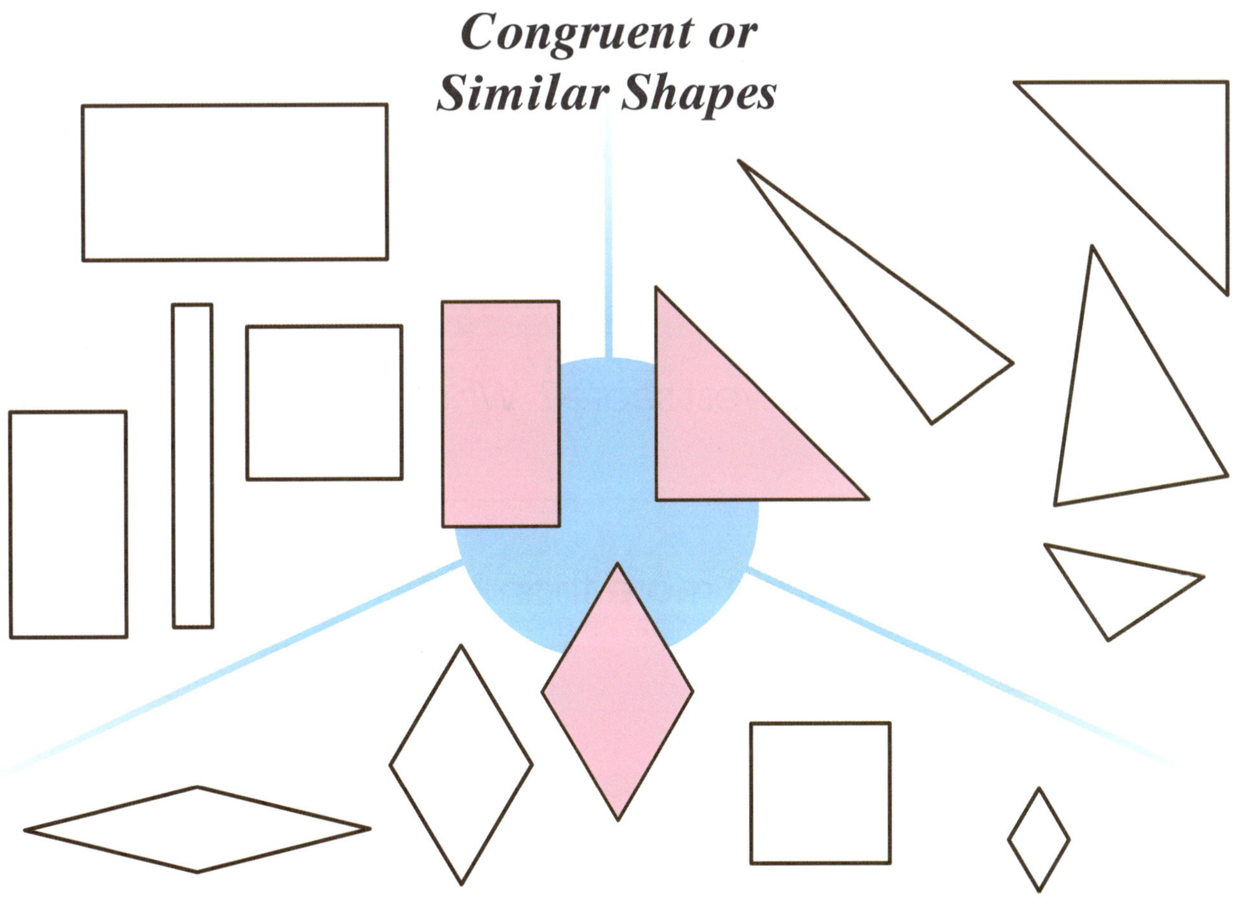

ISBN: 978-1-77149-145-7

D. Look at the graph showing the children's scores for their drawings. Answer the questions.

1. Who got the highest score? What was the highest score?

   ____________ ; ____________

2. Who got the lowest score? What was the lowest score?

   ____________ ; ____________

3. Who got 5 marks more than Ivy?

   ____

4. How many children got a mark below 65?

   ____

ISBN: 978-1-77149-145-7

E. **The children's teacher, Mrs. Louis, gave each child a sticker. Look at the children's stickers. Help them draw the images.**

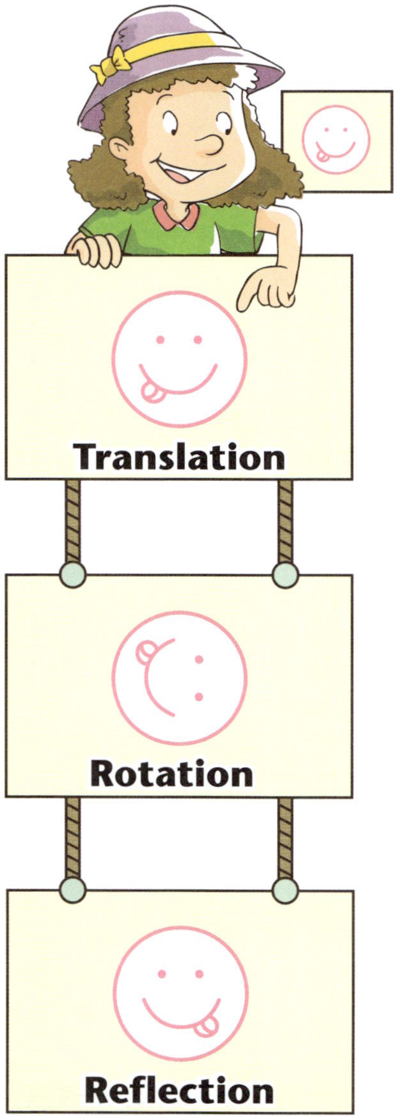

Image	Translation	Rotation	Reflection

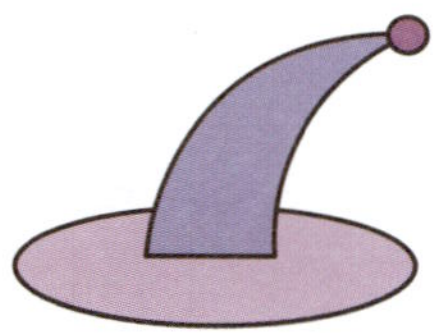			

ISBN: 978-1-77149-145-7

Week 3

Science

A. Look at the pictures. Label each structure as "stable" or "unstable".

1.

2.

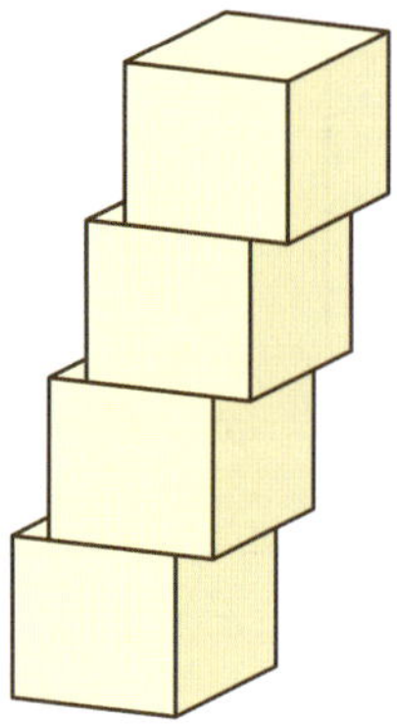

a. ____________ b. ____________

3.

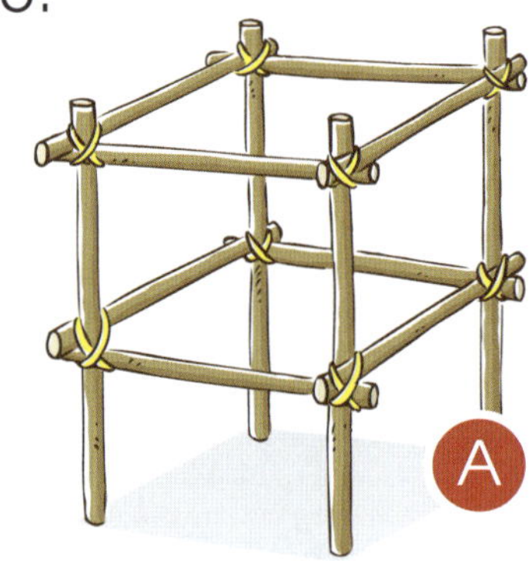

A ____________

B ____________

4.

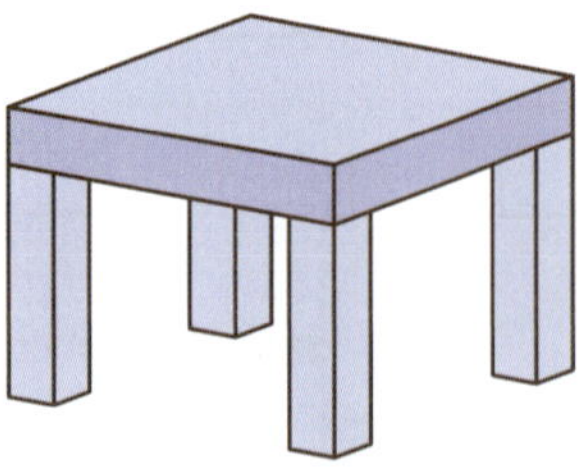

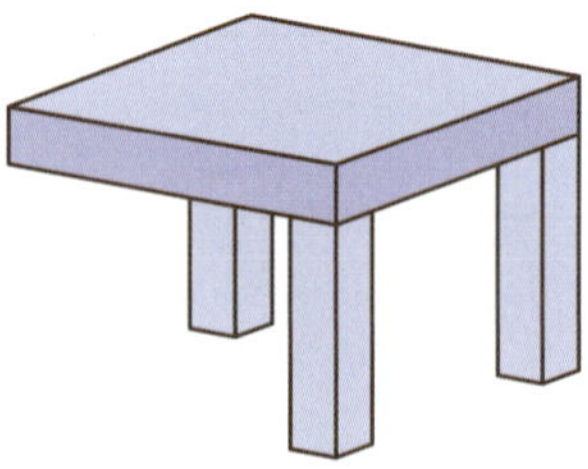

a. ____________ b. ____________

ISBN: 978-1-77149-145-7

B. Write the effect of the force at work in each picture on the line.

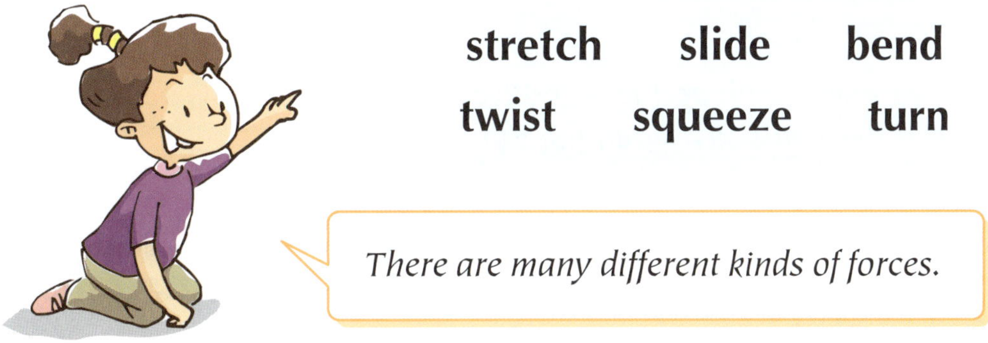

stretch **slide** **bend**
twist **squeeze** **turn**

1. 

____

2. 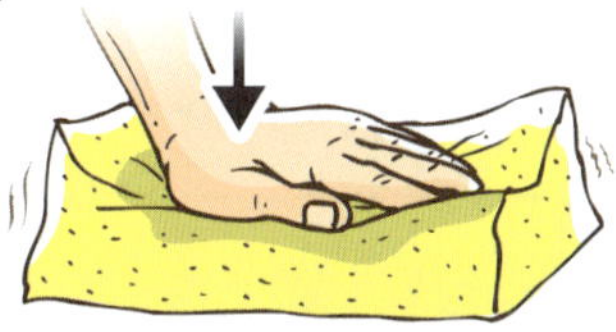

____

3. 

____

4. 

____

5. 

____

6. 

____

ISBN: 978-1-77149-145-7

A. **Read what the girl says. Label the map and answer the questions.**

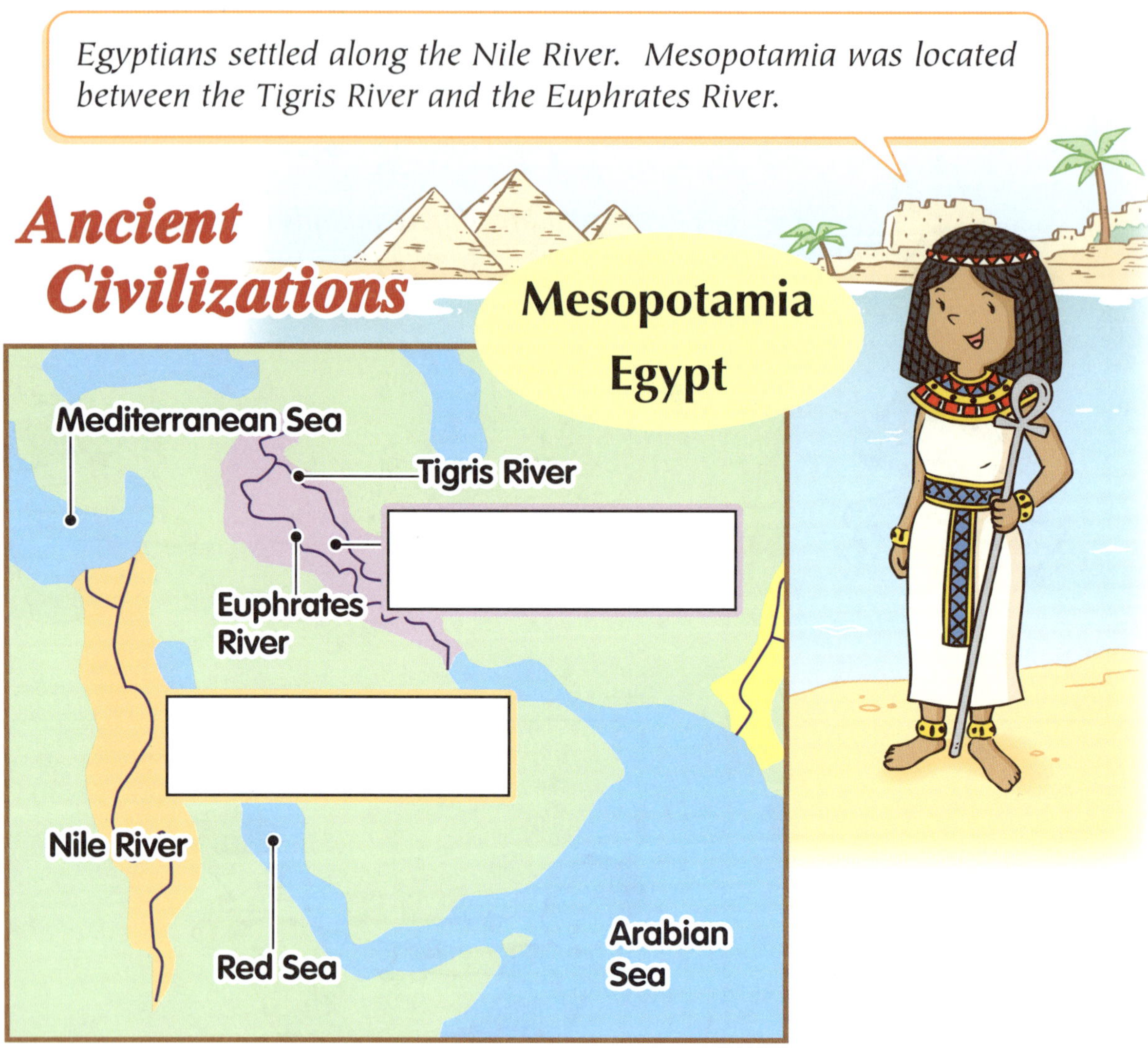

1. What is common between the locations of the ancient Egyptian and Mesopotamian settlements?

____

2. Give one reason why people in the past chose to live along the rivers.

____

Week 3 Social Studies

ISBN: 978-1-77149-145-7

B. Look at the tools and materials used in ancient Egypt for making buildings. Fill in the blanks. Then answer the question.

Materials

Bricks

1. ____________ from the banks of the Nile River was collected and put in a 2. ____________ to make bricks of equal size.

Stones

A 3. ____________ and 4. ____________ were used to break stones into smaller pieces for construction.

Rocks

A 5. ____________ was placed within a crack in rock. It expanded when saturated with water and broke the rock.

List the natural materials used by the ancient Egyptians.

____

ISBN: 978-1-77149-145-7

ISBN: 978-1-77149-145-7

WEEK 4

Arts & Crafts

- make a cosmic mobile

Comics

- The Magic Show

Fun Places to Go in Summer

- Rock Climbing in Whistler

Week 4

ISBN: 978-1-77149-145-7

Week 4

Arts & Crafts

Cosmic Mobile

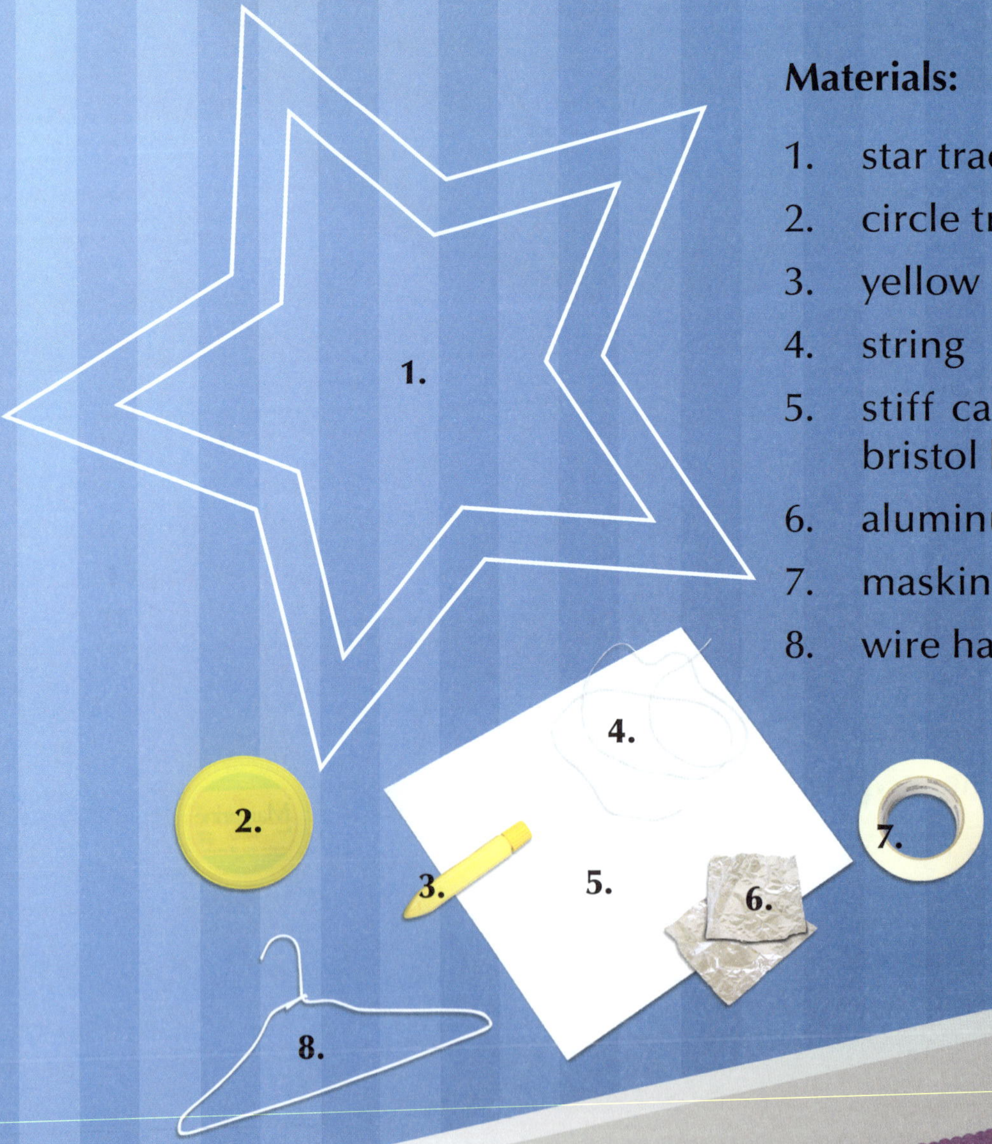

Materials:

1. star tracers
2. circle tracers
3. yellow paint
4. string
5. stiff cardboard or bristol board
6. aluminum foil
7. masking tape
8. wire hanger

ISBN: 978-1-77149-145-7

Directions:

1. Pull wire hanger into circular shape.
2. Using star and circle tracers, trace stars and circles on bristol board or cardboard.
3. Cut some of the large circles into quarter moons and half moons.
4. Cover stars with foil.
5. Paint moons yellow. Let them dry.
6. Attach moons and stars to wire hanger with string.

ISBN: 978-1-77149-145-7

COMICS

The Magic Show

Bill loved video games. He played them every day. His favourite game was "Catch the Rabbit". He had to catch all the white rabbits to win.

One day, Bill's dad asked Bill to go to a magic show with him.

Bill did not want to go. But his dad was firm. So Bill went with him and brought his video game along.

ISBN: 978-1-77149-145-7

ISBN: 978-1-77149-145-7

Suddenly, all of the rabbits from the game hopped toward Bill.

The rabbits chased Bill. The audience laughed.

ISBN: 978-1-77149-145-7

ISBN: 978-1-77149-145-7

Rock Climbing *in Whistler*

Rock climbing is a fun and challenging activity – and where better to try it than on Canada's most renowned mountainous range in Whistler, British Columbia?

The personalized rock climbing program at Whistler caters to people of different ages and levels of experience, and rest assured that the friendly staff will guide you every step of the way. Learn the basics of climbing in a fun atmosphere, through games and activities. Then, let the excitement wash over you as you prepare for your first outdoor climb!

The feeling of tackling a mountain under the warm summer sun is surreal. Test your physical abilities and endurance, and see how far you can go! You may surprise yourself with what you can accomplish with effort and willpower. While you are enjoying your climb, make sure to appreciate the special and unique backdrop of Whistler – it will make your day even more memorable!

ISBN: 978-1-77149-145-7

WEEK 5

English

- read a passage and answer questions
- find synonyms
- write your own story
- use contractions

Mathematics

- draw shapes
- name solids and count the faces
- complete patterns
- round numbers

Science

- understand how rocks become soil
- learn about compost

Social Studies

- learn about the Haudenosaunee creation story
- learn how the Haudenosaunees treat Mother Earth

ISBN: 978-1-77149-145-7

A. Read the passage. Then answer the questions.

It was summer vacation, the time for new adventures, the time to see new places, and the time to make memories that would last a lifetime. There were so many things I wanted to do.

What I Didn't Do During My Summer Vacation

I wanted to go whitewater rafting on the Ottawa River, but my mother said it was too dangerous, so I didn't go. I wanted to swim across Lake Ontario, but my swimming coach told me that I would have to be able to swim across a pool first. I couldn't, so I didn't swim across Lake Ontario. I wanted to fly to Nepal and climb Mount Everest, the tallest mountain in the world. My teacher told me that it would take too long and I would miss too many days of school, so I didn't climb Mount Everest.

During my summer vacation, I didn't do a lot of the things I wanted to do. I did, however, go camping and I stayed in a cottage on Pigeon Lake for a week. I did spend an entire day at Canada's Wonderland. I spent many hours rollerblading, biking, hiking, and splashing in the pool with my friends. During my summer vacation, I had new adventures, I saw new places, and I created memories that would last a lifetime.

ISBN: 978-1-77149-145-7

1. Why did the writer not go whitewater rafting?

____

2. Why did the writer not swim across Lake Ontario?

____

3. What is so special about Mount Everest?

____

4. Name one thing that the writer actually did during her summer vacation.

____

5. *Do you think the writer enjoyed her summer vacation? Why?*

____

____

B. Find the synonyms* of the following words in the passage.

*Synonyms are words that mean the same thing.

1. holiday ____________
2. skip ____________
3. cycling ____________
4. made ____________
5. instructor ____________
6. whole ____________
7. highest ____________
8. unsafe ____________

ISBN: 978-1-77149-145-7

C. **Think about your summer vacation and complete the lists.**

Things I Wanted to Do	Things I Actually Did

D. **Using the information from your lists above, write your own story about your summer vacation.**

What I Didn't Do During My Summer Vacation

ISBN: 978-1-77149-145-7

E. Rewrite each sentence by changing the underlined word(s) into a contraction.

1. I cannot play street hockey this afternoon.

   ____

2. Maria could not find her sunglasses.

   ____

3. I have read stories about Mount Everest.

   ____

4. We are going camping in Algonquin Park.

   ____

F. Complete the statements. Then draw pictures to go with them. Try to make your statements funny.

During my summer vacation, I really wanted to climb Mount Everest. Instead, I climbed a tree in my backyard.

During my summer vacation, I really wanted to ______________

____

Instead, I ______________________________

____

ISBN: 978-1-77149-145-7

A. Read what the children say and draw the shapes on the dot grids.

I want to draw a quadrilateral with 4 equal sides, but it is not a square.

I like parallelograms. I want to draw a parallelogram with 4 right angles.

David says, "I want to draw a polygon with 3 sides. It has 1 right angle."

Leon says, "I want to draw a quadrilateral. It looks like a ladder."

Sue says, "I want to draw a 3-sided polygon. 2 of the sides have the same length."

Linda

Mary

David

Leon

Sue

ISBN: 978-1-77149-145-7

B. Look at the solids the children made. Help them name the solids and find the number of faces on each shape.

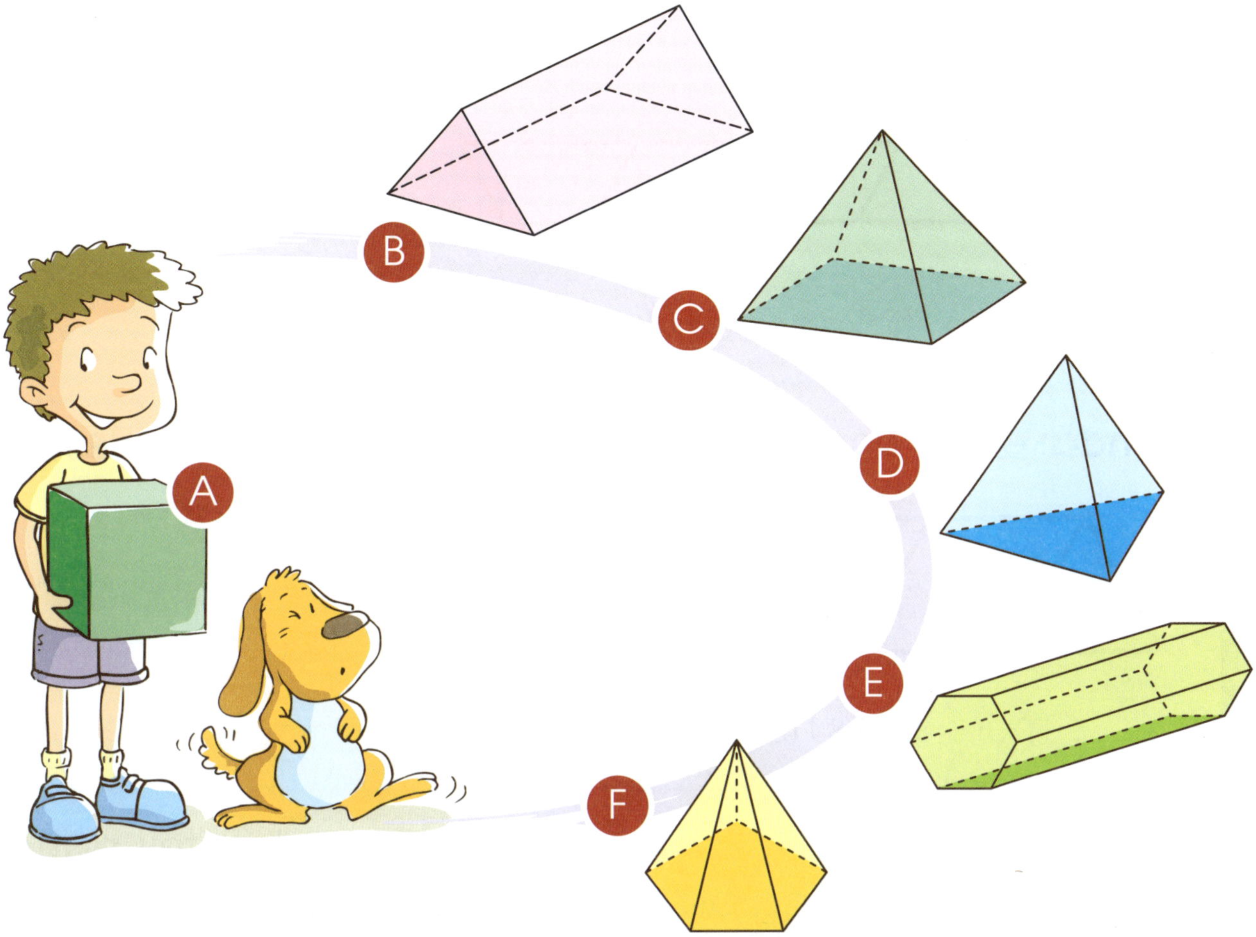

	Name	No. of Faces
A		
B		
C		
D		
E		
F		

ISBN: 978-1-77149-145-7

C. The children glue sticks to form patterns. Help each child continue the pattern and find how many more sticks are needed.

Leon: extending this pattern to 9 congruent trapezoids

_____ more sticks needed

Linda: extending this pattern to 8 congruent triangles

_____ more sticks needed

Mary: extending this pattern to 9 congruent rhombuses

_____ more sticks needed

Sue: extending this pattern to 16 congruent triangles

_____ more sticks needed

ISBN: 978-1-77149-145-7

D. See how many shapes the children cut out. Help them write the numbers in expanded form and round them to the nearest 10. Then write the rounded numbers in words to complete what they say.

82 shapes

Expanded form: 80 + 2

Rounded to the nearest 10: ______

I've cut out about ________ shapes.

68 shapes

Expanded form: ____________

Rounded to the nearest 10: ______

I've cut out about ________ shapes.

47 shapes

Expanded form: ____________

Rounded to the nearest 10: ______

I've cut out about ________ shapes.

59 shapes

Expanded form: ____________

Rounded to the nearest 10: ______

I've cut out about ________ shapes.

ISBN: 978-1-77149-145-7

A. Fill in the blanks to complete the paragraph. Then label the diagram.

Do you know how the weather helps make soil?

bigger crack soil cold

Weather & Soil

When the weather gets hot, rocks become 1. __________ . When the weather gets 2. __________ , rocks become smaller. If this happens often enough, the rocks will 3. __________ and break up into smaller pieces. When they get really small, they turn into 4. __________ .

From Rocks to Soil

small pieces
soil
rocks

____

____

____

Science Fun

The rock in soil has been broken down over millions of years to the size of sand, or smaller. Silt is smaller than sand, and clay is even smaller!

ISBN: 978-1-77149-145-7

B. Fill in the blanks to complete the paragraph about compost. Then see what we might put into a compost bin. Circle the words in the word search.

compost **humus** **decaying**

__________ in soil is good for growing plants because of the nutrients that it contains. In nature, humus is made from __________ plants or animal remains. We make humus when we __________ .

vegetables **grass**
plants **fruit** **tea bags**
leaves **egg shells**
soil **coffee grounds**

t	k	e	g	g	s	h	e	l	l	s	g	w
e	w	h	v	e	g	e	t	a	b	l	e	s
a	b	v	q	a	d	s	f	t	w	n	v	l
b	l	s	o	i	l	y	g	l	f	u	l	e
a	c	n	c	z	f	r	u	i	t	g	j	a
g	r	a	s	s	s	m	v	w	m	r	p	v
s	z	v	j	z	p	l	a	n	t	s	k	e
c	o	f	f	e	e	g	r	o	u	n	d	s

ISBN: 978-1-77149-145-7

Week 5

Social Studies

A. Fill in the blanks to learn about the Haudenosaunee creation story.

The Haudenosaunee *Creation Story*

island good
plants water
otter corn
turtle

In the beginning, there was only Sky World. There was w__________ everywhere in the world below.

One day, a pregnant Sky Woman fell from Sky World. She grabbed some p__________ as she fell. Some water birds saved her from the fall. An o__________ brought earth from the ocean's floor and put it on a t__________'s back to form an i__________ . This became Turtle Island.

Sky Woman had a daughter, she grew up and had twin sons. Sadly, she died and was later known as Mother Earth. Sky Woman placed the plants from Sky World on her daughter's grave. Squash, beans, and c__________ grew from it. They are called the Three Sisters.

ISBN: 978-1-77149-145-7

Later Sky Woman died as well and became Grandmother Moon. When the twins grew up, one became the Creator and created the g__________ things on Earth. However, his brother destroyed the things he created and made disturbing things like snakes and earthquakes.

That is how the Haudenosaunees believe the Earth was created!

B. Read the clues and complete the crossword puzzle with words from the story to see what the Elder says.

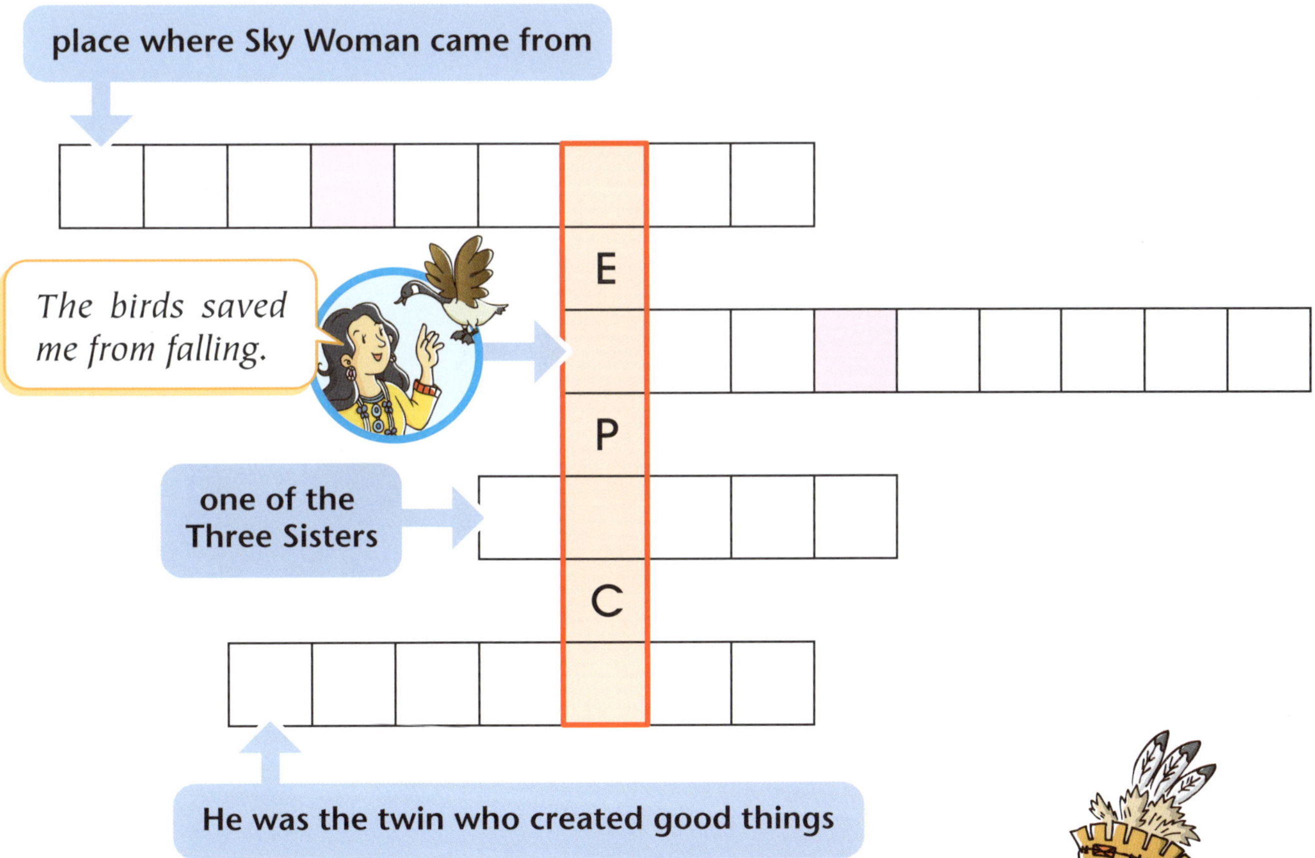

This creation story shows that the Haudenosaunees believe in treating Mother Earth with __________ .

ISBN: 978-1-77149-145-7

ISBN: 978-1-77149-145-7

Week 6

English
- read a passage and answer questions
- use quotation marks
- write an ending to a story
- complete a crossword puzzle

Mathematics
- find the cost and change
- find divisible numbers
- write whole numbers and fractions
- complete and describe number patterns

Science
- learn about friction between different surfaces
- identify whether objects "grip" or "slip"

Social Studies
- name the provinces and territories of Canada
- learn about animals specific to the provinces and territories

* The Canadian penny is no longer in circulation. It is used in the unit to show money amounts to the cent.

ISBN: 978-1-77149-145-7

A. Read the passage. Then answer the questions.

Larry's Adventure in the Castle

Larry sat at the back of the yellow school bus. It was a very bumpy ride, but it was worth it. Today, Larry's class was visiting a real castle.

The bus finally came to a stop in front of a magnificent building. Larry could not believe his eyes. The castle was identical to the ones that he had been studying in class.

Mr. Pitterson greeted the students on the stairs. He was going to lead the tour through the castle. He explained to the students that they would be seeing many old and interesting artifacts. He also warned them not to wander off alone because it was very easy to get lost in this old, enormous building.

Larry was not listening. He was far too busy staring at something standing at the end of a long corridor. Larry slowly moved closer to examine the object. It was a large, silver suit of armour. Beside the armour was a closed door with a large sign. On the sign were the words, "DO NOT ENTER". Larry felt his hand moving toward the doorknob...

ISBN: 978-1-77149-145-7

1. How does the writer describe the trip to the castle?

2. Why did Mr. Pitterson tell the children not to wander off alone?

3. What caught Larry's attention in the castle?

4. Write out a sentence from the story that shows that Larry was very curious.

B. Add quotation marks to the following sentences.

1. The teacher said, The castle is very old and historic.
2. Let's go into this room! shouted Larry.
3. How long will the bus ride be? asked the class.
4. I enjoyed the trip, said Brian.

ISBN: 978-1-77149-145-7

C. **Using the following questions to guide you, write an exciting ending to the story. Draw a picture to go with it and suggest a new title for the story.**

- What adventure lay behind the closed door?
- What happened to Larry?
- How did Larry get back to his classmates?

New Title

ISBN: 978-1-77149-145-7

D. Read the clues and complete the crossword puzzle with words from the passage.

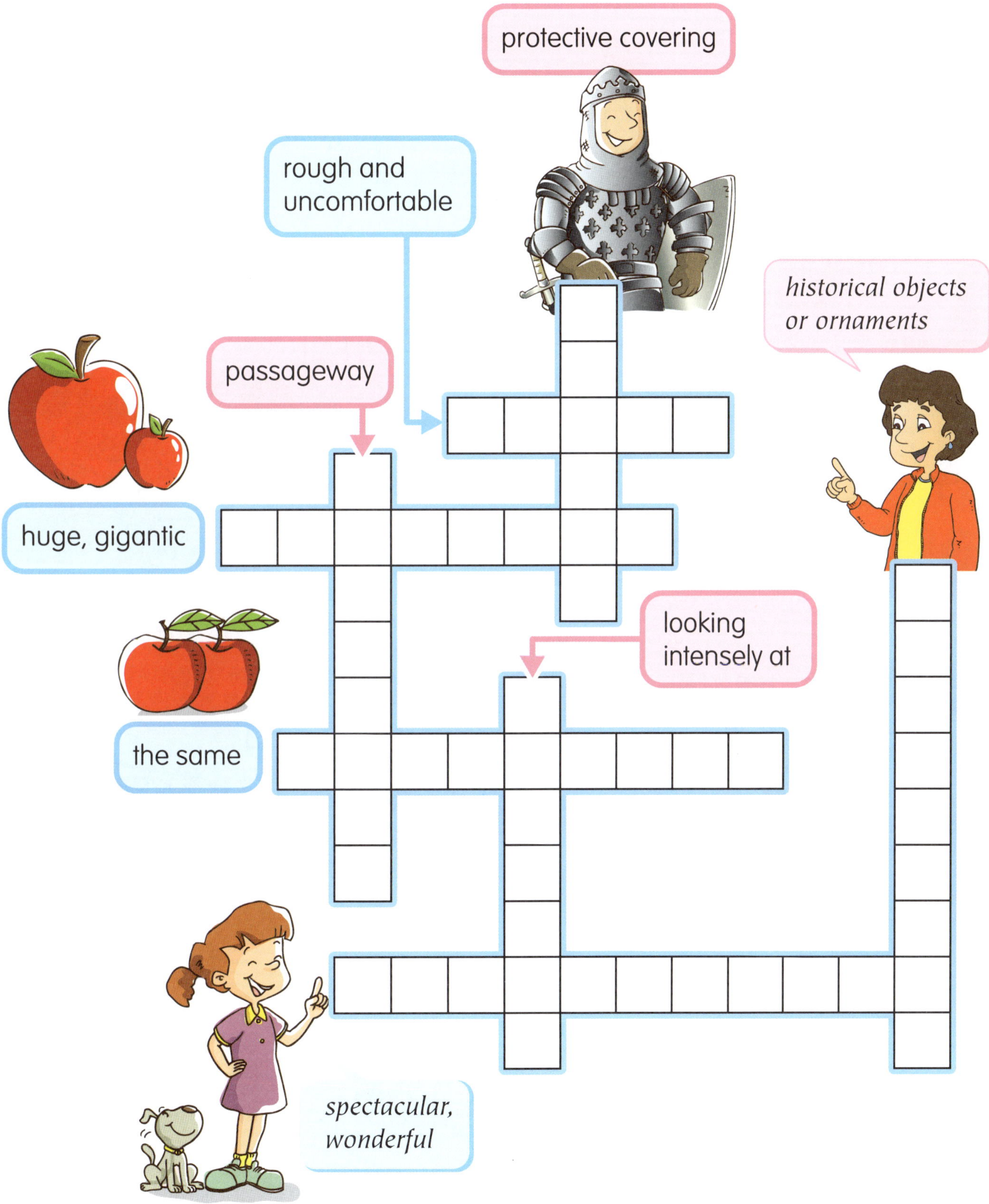

ISBN: 978-1-77149-145-7

Week 6

Mathematics

A. Look at the objects. Help the cashier write the prices in decimals. Then find the cost and the change in each situation.

1.

$ ______ each

4 dollars 60 cents

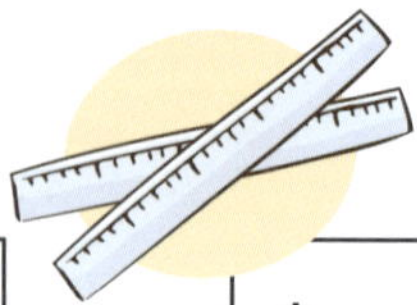

$ ______ each

95 cents

$ ______ each

1 dollar 9 cents

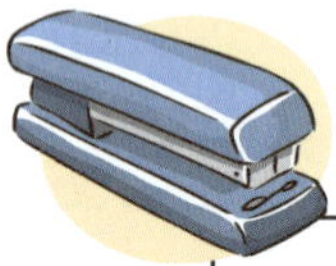

$ ______ each

4 dollars 49 cents

$ ______ each

3 dollars 60 cents

$ ______ each

2 dollars 89 cents

2.

Cost: $ __________

Pay:

Change: $ ________

3.

Cost: $ __________

Pay:

Change: $ ________

4.

Cost: $ __________

Pay:

Change: $ ________

ISBN: 978-1-77149-145-7

B. Lucy got some raffle tickets from buying the items. Colour the tickets and do the skill-testing questions. Then answer the question.

A Colour the numbers that are divisible by 5.

30	99	90	63	22	25	55	40
10	43	35	108	49	68	84	85
20	15	5	70	457	75	45	60
32	72	80	503	9	100	752	37
356	102	65	6	207	95	50	105

Skill-testing Questions:

465 + 296 = ______

510 + 114 = ______

327 – 285 = ______

B Colour the numbers that are divisible by 2.

81	24	30	42	3
11	2	13	83	43
27	10	6	28	87
0	14	37	44	9
5	38	26	50	15

Skill-testing Questions:

6 x 5 = ______

2 x 7 = ______

4 x 9 = ______

C Colour the numbers that are divisible by 10.

32	10	50	40	42
13	25	22	60	8
34	30	70	80	93
62	20	36	31	72
36	150	100	90	39

Skill-testing Questions:

700 – 85 = ______

663 – 319 = ______

511 + 206 = ______

If the hidden number in the puzzle is the same as one of the answers to the skill-testing questions, I can get a prize. Which ticket can win a prize?

Ticket ______ can win a prize.

ISBN: 978-1-77149-145-7

C. **Look at the stickers that Elaine bought. Help her write whole numbers or fractions to complete the sentences.**

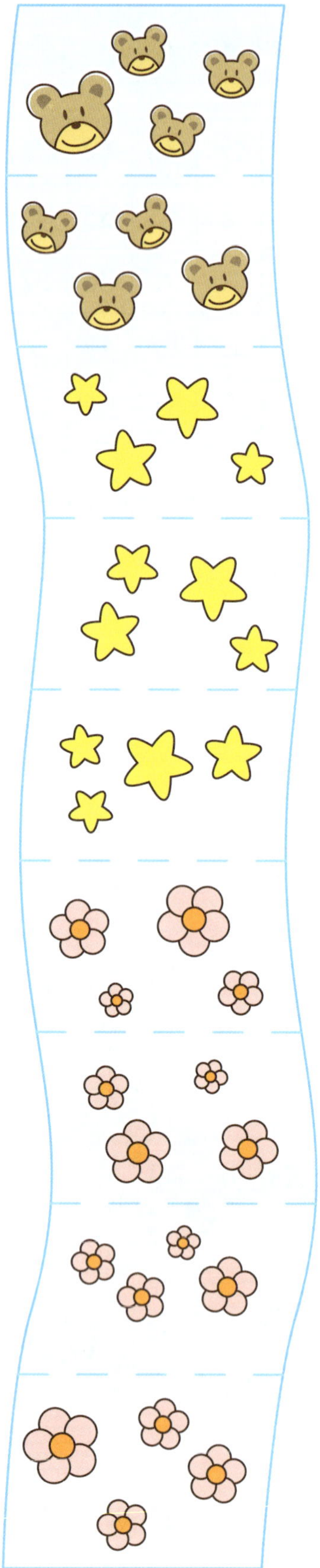

1. There are 9 groups of ______ stickers; there are ______ stickers in all.

2. 8 out of ______ stickers are bears.

   ☐ of a sheet of stickers are bears.

3. ______ out of ______ stickers are stars.

   ☐ of a sheet of stickers are stars.

4. If Elaine divides the stars into 2 equal groups, there would be ______ stars in each group.

5. *If I give $\frac{1}{2}$ of my sheet of stickers to Lucy, how many stickers will she get?*

______ stickers

ISBN: 978-1-77149-145-7

D. Elaine is writing numbers on her sticker sheets. Follow the patterns to complete the sequences and describe the patterns.

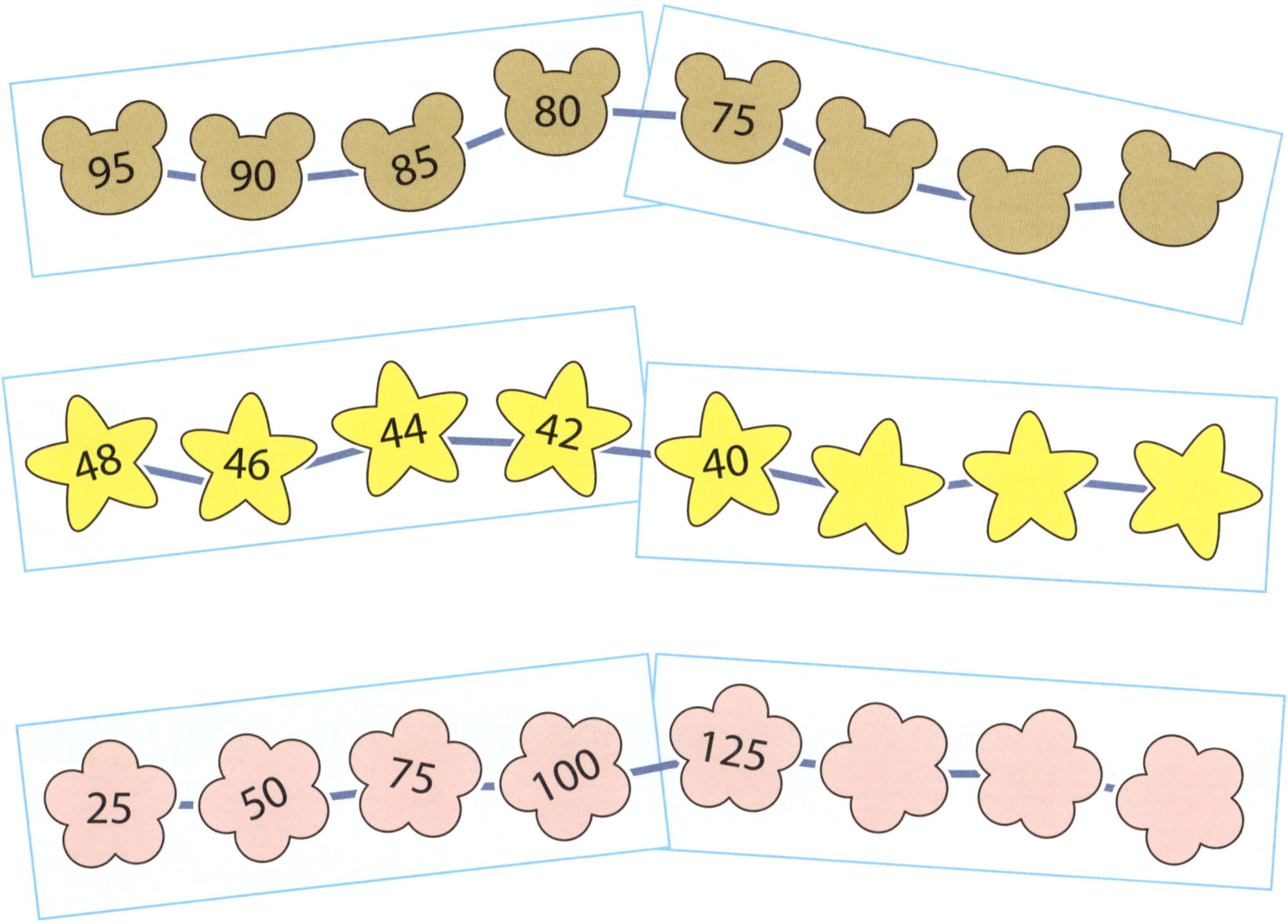

Number Pattern

 : The numbers **increase / decrease** by ________ each time.

 : ____

 : ____

ISBN: 978-1-77149-145-7

Week 6

Science

A. Complete the sentences with the given words.

more　　rough　　force　　friction　　less

1. The bottoms of hiking boots are ________ so that there is a good amount of friction between the boots and the ground.

2. When the tires on a bike become worn down, there is ________ friction between the tires and the road. The bike may skid easily.

3. When we walk across a slippery floor with socks on, there is little ________ and we may slip.

4. When you need one thing to grip another, you need ________ friction.

5. Friction is a ________ that slows down moving things.

ISBN: 978-1-77149-145-7

B. Grip or slip? Things grip if there is enough friction. Write "grip" in the box if there is friction. Write "slip" if there is not.

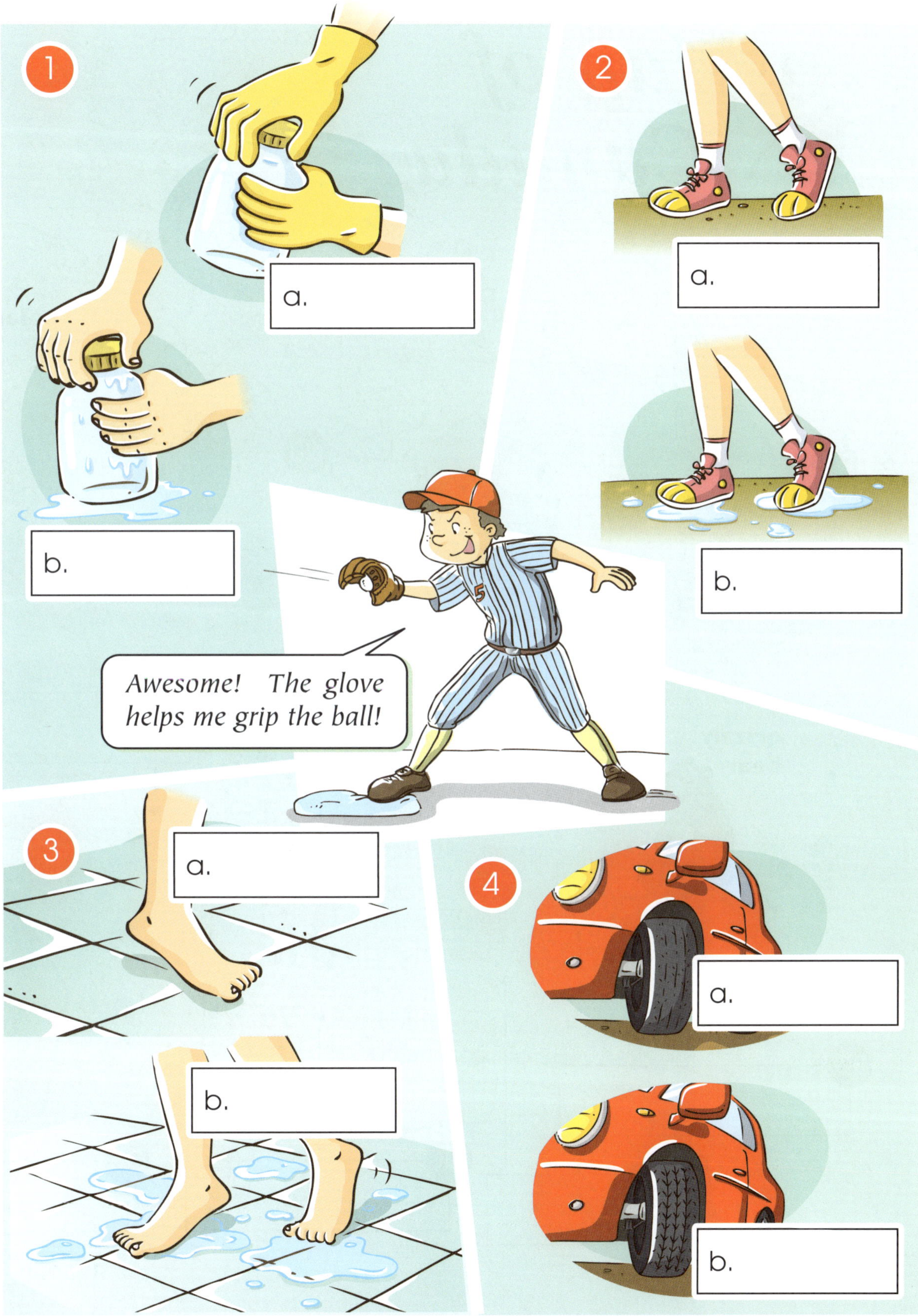

ISBN: 978-1-77149-145-7

Name the provinces and territories of Canada. Then answer the questions.

Map of Canada

Week 6

Social Studies

ISBN: 978-1-77149-145-7

1. The capital of Canada: ____________

2. Mark the area where you live with a 🏠 symbol.

3. Name the province or territory with:

polar bears: ____________ grizzly bears: ____________

caribous: ____________ loons: ____________

snowy owls: ____________ deer: ____________

fish: ____________

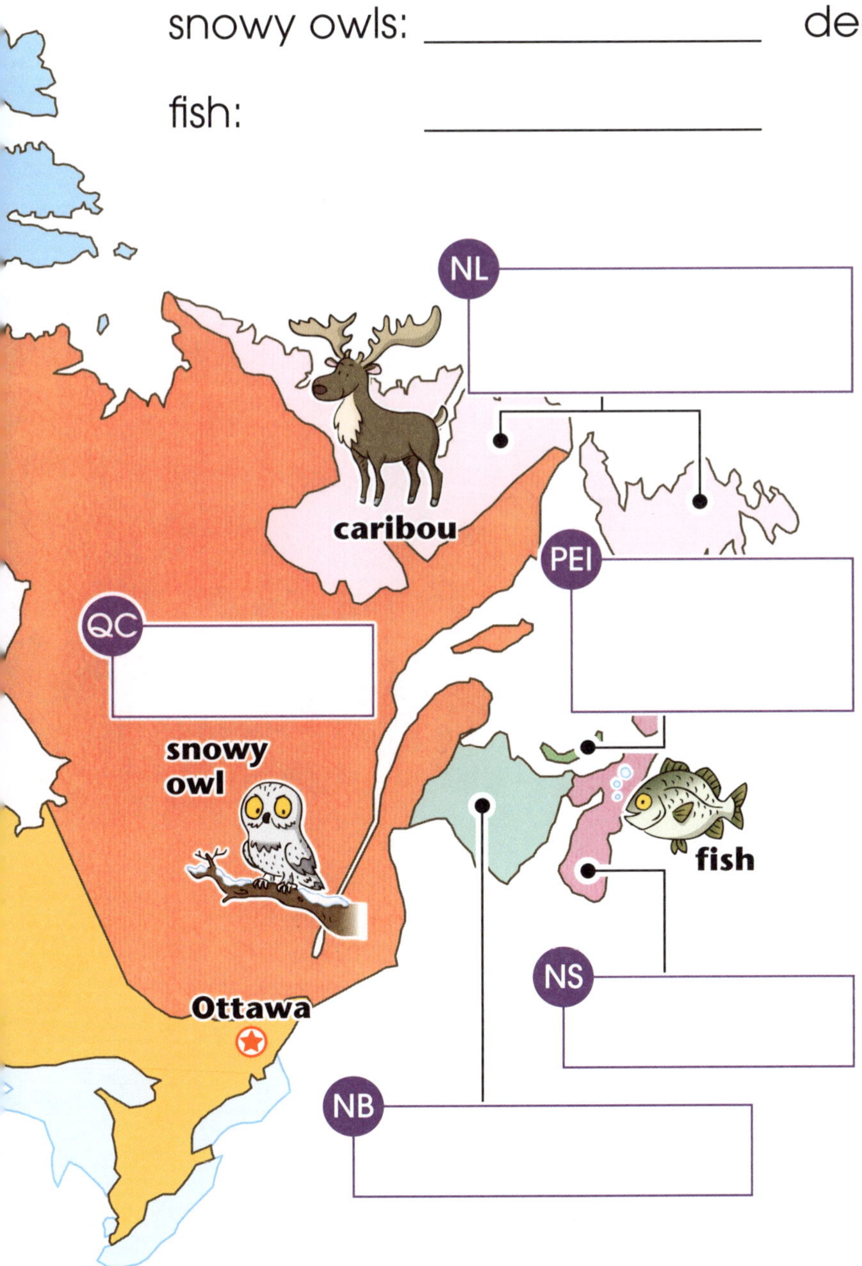

Provinces

AB	Alberta
BC	British Columbia
MB	Manitoba
NB	New Brunswick
NL	Newfoundland and Labrador
NS	Nova Scotia
ON	Ontario
PEI	Prince Edward Island
QC	Quebec
SK	Saskatchewan

Territories

NT	Northwest Territories
NU	Nunavut
YT	Yukon

ISBN: 978-1-77149-145-7

ISBN: 978-1-77149-145-7

Week 7

English

- read a passage
- find antonyms
- write a letter
- write the past tense of verbs

Mathematics

- distinguish possible from impossible events
- understand the outcomes of a spinner
- solve problems involving fractions and probabilities
- find the weight

Science

- review magnets
- show how bar magnets interact with each other

Social Studies

- draw pictures to show the stages of clear-cutting
- learn about the impact of clearing forests

ISBN: 978-1-77149-145-7

A. Read the passage.

The Time Capsule

Daniel could hardly believe his luck. He had been planting trees with his father in the backyard when he suddenly uncovered an unusual container. He opened the container and inside he found some interesting items. The most important item was a letter. It read as follows.

1254 Peach Street
Ottawa, Ontario T6V 3W4
August 14, 1986

Dear Friend,

If you are reading this letter, you have found my time capsule. My name is Sara Burch and I am eleven years old. I have decided to make a time capsule to hold things that represent me and the time I am living in.

I have enclosed a picture of my family. I am the one holding the Cabbage Patch Kid doll. It was difficult to get this doll because they have become so popular. The piece of string shows you my height at the time that I wrote this letter. The candy wrapper is from my favourite candies, Jolly Ranchers. These rectangular candies come in the greatest flavours.

The newspaper article shows a very important moment that will go down in history. This year, the space shuttle Challenger exploded as it took off for space. It was a tragic event, but it will always be remembered.

I have also enclosed a list of my favourite things. As you can see, my favourite singer is Madonna, my favourite movie is "Ghostbusters", and my favourite TV show is "The Care Bears".

I hope you enjoy looking through my time capsule and that you have learned something about the past that you did not already know.

Yours truly,
Sara Burch

ISBN: 978-1-77149-145-7

B. Put a line through the things that were not found in Sara's time capsule.

- a letter
- a drawing
- a photo
- a Care Bear
- a piece of string
- a candy wrapper
- a Cabbage Patch Kid doll
- a newspaper article
- a list of Sara's favourite things

C. Complete the crossword puzzle with the antonyms of the clue words. These words can be found in the passage.

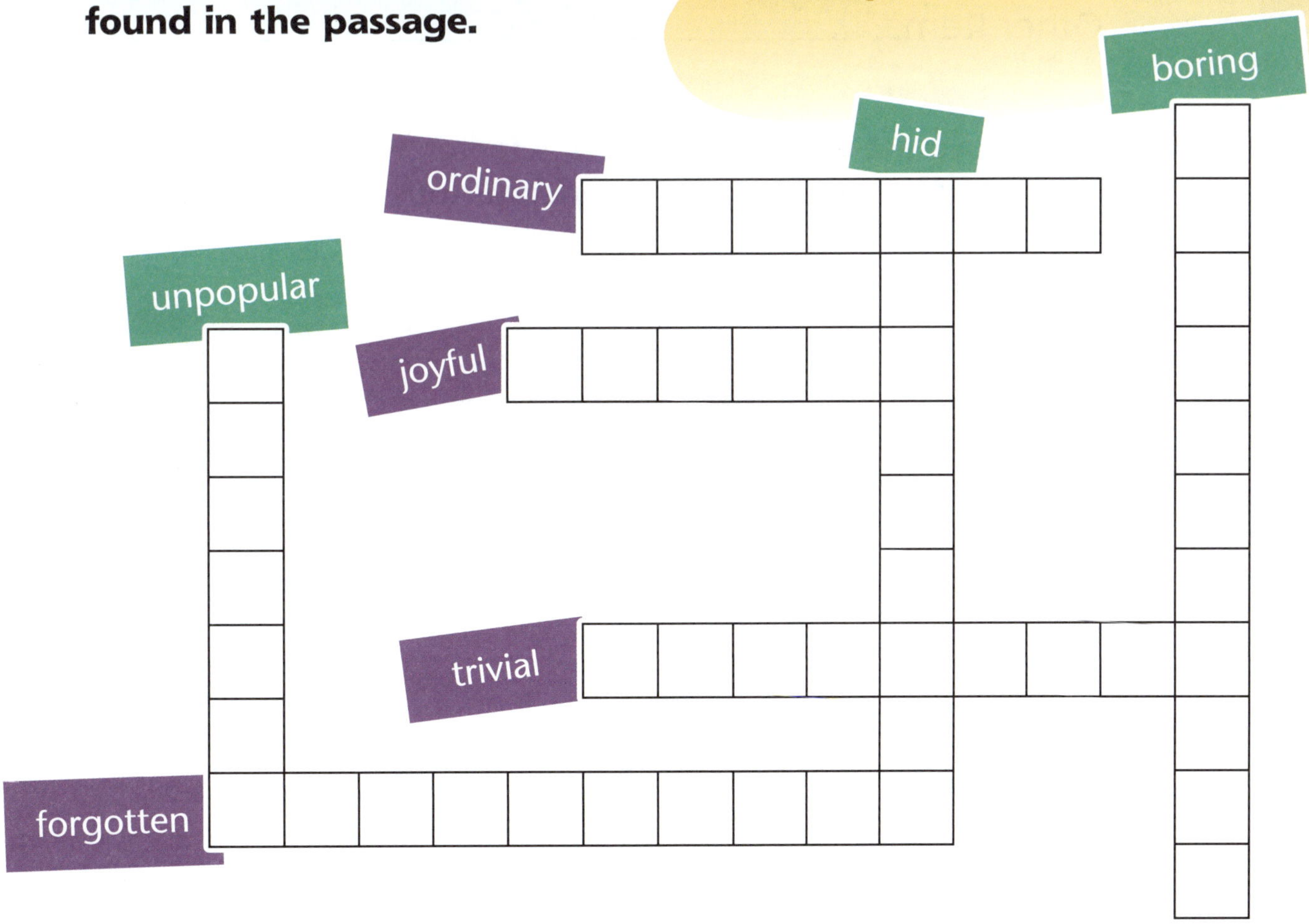

ISBN: 978-1-77149-145-7

D. Pretend that you are going to make a time capsule. Write the things that you would like to share with people in the future.

Toy: ____________________

Singer/Group: ____________________

Movie: ____________________

Food: ____________________

TV Show: ____________________

Major Event: ____________________

Other Items: ____________________

E. Using the list above and Sara's letter to guide you, write a letter to the person who may find your time capsule.

ISBN: 978-1-77149-145-7

F. Rewrite each sentence in the past tense.

1. Dad plants trees in the backyard.

____

2. I need a pen to write the letter.

____

3. My sister plays in the sandbox.

____

4. We laugh at the dog's tricks.

____

5. I follow the path through the forest.

____

G. Match each verb with its past tense form. Write your answers on the lines.

Present Tense	*Past Tense*
drive	____________
dig	____________
write	____________
fly	____________
bring	____________
drink	____________
buy	____________
find	____________

ISBN: 978-1-77149-145-7

Week

7

Mathematics

A. The children are talking about the possibility of some events. Write "possible" or "impossible" on the lines.

1.

I can make 100 L of fresh orange juice in 1 minute.

____

2.

I can finish an apple in 15 minutes.

____

3.

I can score twice today.

____

4.

She will pick a red ball.

a. ________________

I will pick a blue ball.

b. ________________

5.

The leaves will turn green in the winter.

____

ISBN: 978-1-77149-145-7

B. The children are playing with a spinner. Look at the spinner. Help the children trace the correct letter to tell whether the sentence is true (T) or false (F).

The spinner is most likely to land on  .

The spinner is least likely to land on  .

There is a chance that the spinner will land on  .

The spinner will never land on  .

The best word to describe the chance of the spinner landing on  is "impossible".

There is a greater chance that the spinner will land on "Please try again!" than on  .

John says, "The spinner landed on  last time. It won't land on  again."

Elaine says, "If the spinner is spun 20 times, I think it may stop on  5 times."

ISBN: 978-1-77149-145-7

C. Judy is going to let her friends pick a ball from a box of 12 balls. Help her colour the balls. Then answer the questions.

1. *$\frac{5}{12}$ of the balls are green, $\frac{4}{12}$ are yellow, and the rest are red.*

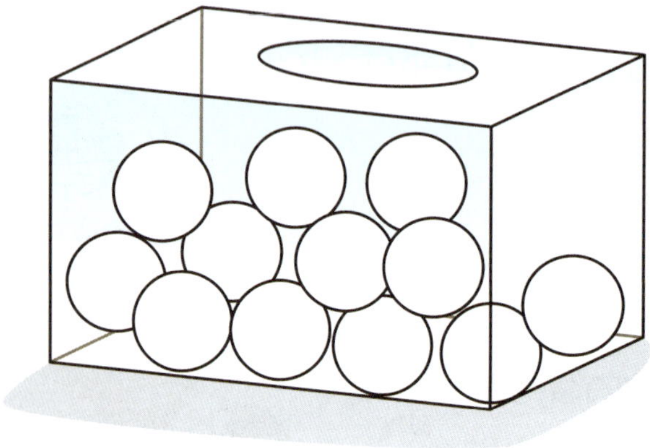

2. Is it possible to pick
   a. a green ball? ____________
   b. a purple ball? ____________

3. Is there a greater chance of picking
   a. a red ball or a yellow ball? ____________
   b. a yellow ball or a green ball? ____________

4. If Judy divides the balls equally into 2 bags and puts all the yellow ones in one bag, how can the balls be divided? Show two possible combinations.

1st Combination

Bag 1: 4 yellow + ______ green

Bag 2: ______ green + ______ red

2nd Combination

Bag 1: 4 yellow + ____________

Bag 2: ____________

ISBN: 978-1-77149-145-7

D. Judy weighs her toys using marbles. See how much each type of marble weighs. Then help Judy record the weight of the items and answer the questions.

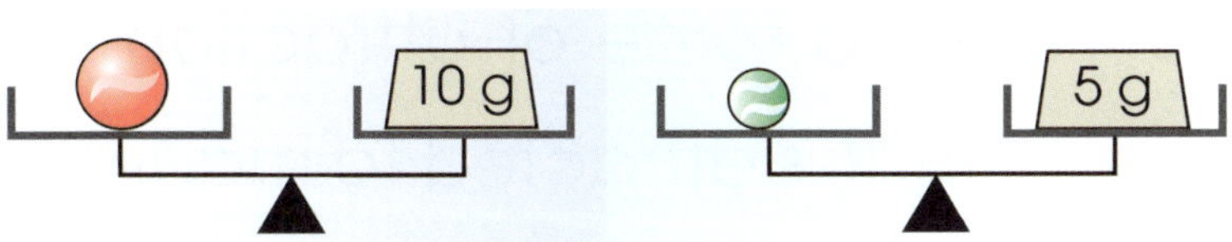

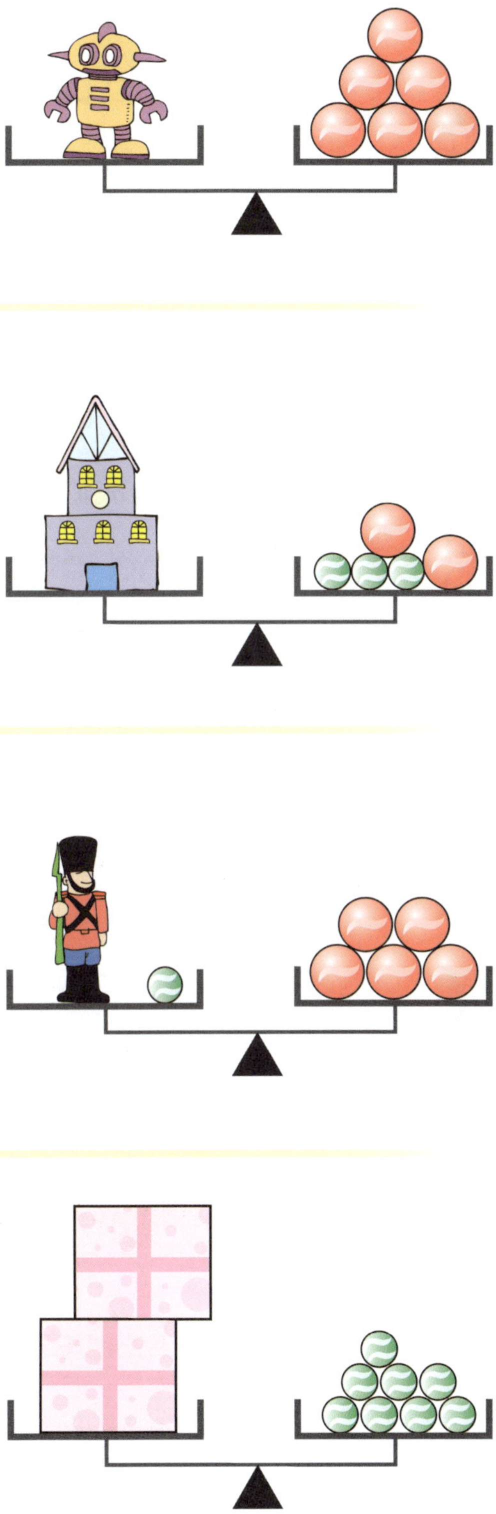

1. ***Weight***

   Robot: __________

   House: __________

   Soldier: __________

   Gift Box: __________

2. What is the weight of 3 soldiers?

   ____

3. What is the total weight of 1 house and 1 gift box?

   ____

4. The vase weighs 95 g. Draw the fewest marbles needed to balance the vase.

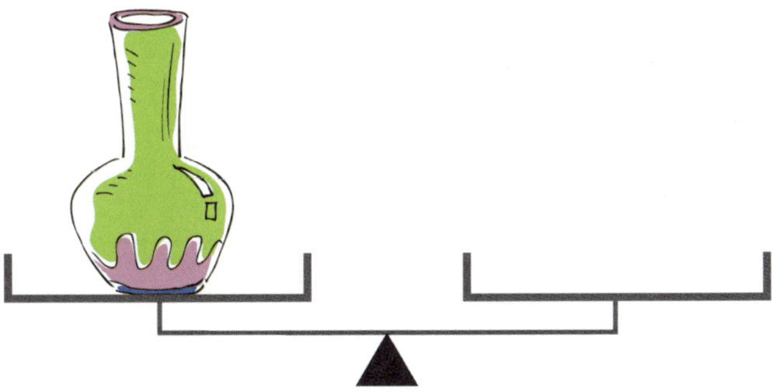

ISBN: 978-1-77149-145-7

A. Circle the correct words to complete the paragraphs about magnets. Then label the ends of the bar magnet.

Magnets / Plastics exert a force of attraction on some metals. A material that is attracted to magnets is said to be **magic / magnetic** . For something to be magnetic, it must be made of **iron / plastic** , nickel, or cobalt.

A bar magnet has **two / three** ends. If you tie a string to the middle of a bar magnet, the end of the magnet that points north is called the **west / north** pole and the other end pointing south is called the **south / east** pole.

ISBN: 978-1-77149-145-7

B. Fill in the blanks to complete the sentences. Then label the ends of the magnets.

Properties of a Magnet

repels	attracts
like	unlike

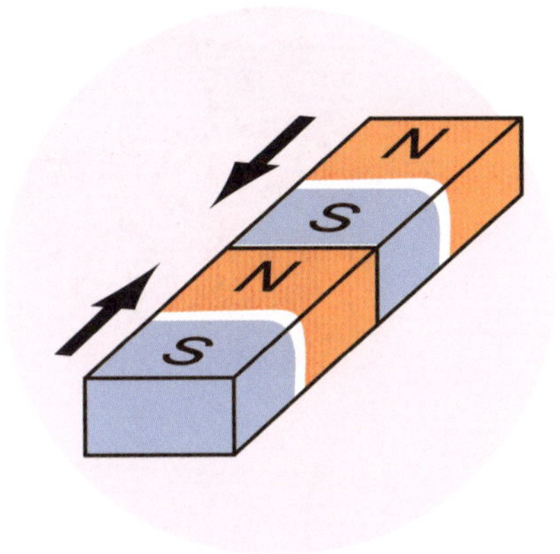

The south pole of a magnet 1. ____________ the north pole of another magnet.

2. ____________ poles attract each other.

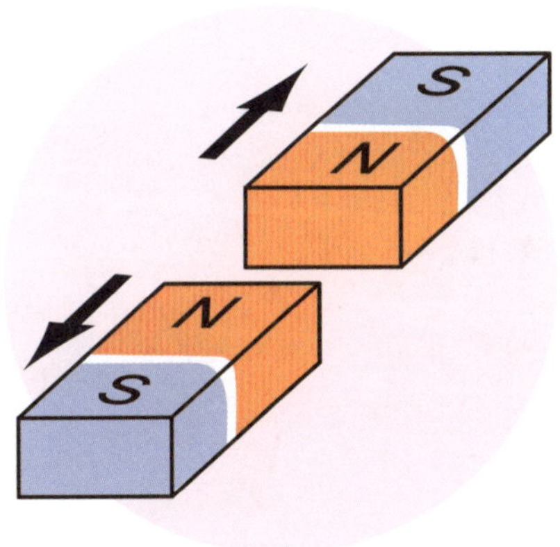

The north pole of a magnet 3. ____________ the north pole of another magnet.

4. ____________ poles repel each other.

5. Write "N" for north and "S" for south in the circles.

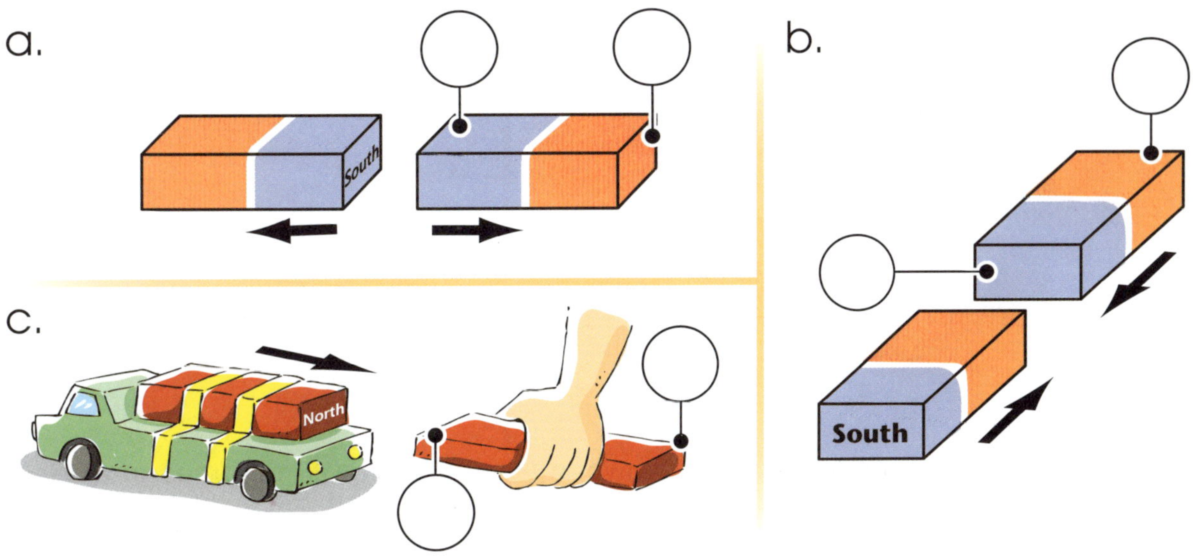

ISBN: 978-1-77149-145-7

A. Name and draw to complete the different stages of clear-cutting.

Clear-cutting is the cutting down of trees in an area. One purpose is to regenerate the area with new, healthier trees.

Stages	Symbols
replantation	cut down tree stump
natural forest	small plant
clear-cut area	big tree
human-made forest	animals

Clear-cutting in Canada

Stage 1: ____________________

different types of trees and lots of animals

Stage 2: ____________________

an area with cut down tree stumps only

Stage 3: ____________________

an area with small plants in rows; a few animals

Stage 4: ____________________

an area with big trees in rows; more animals

ISBN: 978-1-77149-145-7

B. Forests are also cleared for the development of tourism. Read what the environmentalist and the businessman say. Then answer the questions.

1. List one positive and one negative impacts of tourism.

   Positive: ______________________________

   ____

   Negative: ______________________________

   ____

2. Do you think forests should be cleared for tourism? Why?

   ____

   ____

ISBN: 978-1-77149-145-7

ISBN: 978-1-77149-145-7

WEEK 8

Arts & Crafts

- make marshmallow bunnies

Comics

- Gifts from the Old Man

Fun Places to Go in Summer

- Mont Saint-Sauveur Water Park

ISBN: 978-1-77149-145-7

Marshmallow Bunnies

Directions:

1. Glue 2 large marshmallows together as shown.
2. Put toothpick through 1 small marshmallow on each side for arms.
3. Put toothpick through 2 small marshmallows for each ear.
4. Cut out inside of ears from construction paper and glue them onto marshmallow ears.
5. Put toothpick through 1 small marshmallow for bunny tail.
6. Glue chocolate chips onto face for eyes.

ISBN: 978-1-77149-145-7

Materials for 1 Bunny:

- 2 large marshmallows
- 7 small marshmallows
- toothpicks
- construction paper
- 2 chocolate chips
- thin red licorice
- glue

7. Glue small marshmallow for nose.
8. Cut licorice to 2 cm (x 6) and glue it around marshmallow nose.

ISBN: 978-1-77149-145-7

COMICS

Gifts from the Old Man

ISBN: 978-1-77149-145-7

ISBN: 978-1-77149-145-7

The greedy goldsmith stroked his gold. He wanted to have more.

That night, the goldsmith returned to the hilltop. Again, the old man cut the goldsmith's hair.

The old man nodded silently.

ISBN: 978-1-77149-145-7

ISBN: 978-1-77149-145-7

Mont Saint-Sauveur *Water Park*

Is the scorching sun making you hide indoors this summer? There is a better way to beat the heat: head over to Mont Saint-Sauveur Water Park!

Located in Saint-Sauveur, Quebec – just 45 minutes from Montreal – Mont Saint-Sauveur contains all the fun and excitement you would expect from a great water park. There are thrilling waterslides, wave pools, artificial beaches, and much more!

This water park is actually a ski resort in the winter. Therefore, there are some unusual rides that you would not normally see at a water park. Don't miss out on the alpine coaster that follows a track down the mountain and takes you through the beautiful scenery. For those who meet the height requirements, there are even waterslides on the mountain that start so high up that you need to take ski lifts to get to the top!

Mont Saint-Sauveur truly gives you a one-of-a-kind water park experience!

ISBN: 978-1-77149-145-7

Answers

Grades 3-4

Credits

Photos ("children" Gennadiy Poznyakov/123RF.com, "beach" Alexandr Ozerov/123RF.com)

ISBN: 978-1-77149-145-7

ANSWERS

Week 1

English

B. A magician usually wears a top hat.
C. 2 ; 3 ; 1 ; 4 ; 5
D. (Individual answers)
E. (Individual writing)
F.

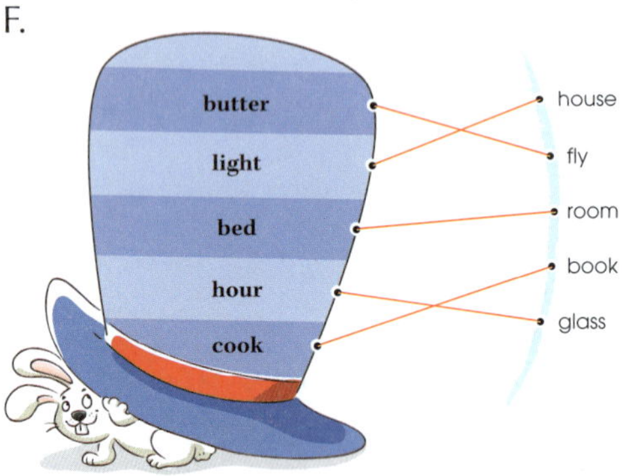

Mathematics

A. John: 80 ; 81 ; 82 ; 83 ; 84
Peter: 85 ; 90 ; 95 ; 100 ; 105
Lucy: 92 ; 94 ; 96 ; 98 ; 100
Sue: 50 ; 75 ; 100 ; 125 ; 150
Sue

B. 1.
$$\begin{array}{r} 500 \\ -\ 427 \\ \hline 73 \end{array}$$
; 73

2.
$$\begin{array}{r} 273 \\ +\ 185 \\ \hline 458 \end{array}$$
; 458

3.
$$\begin{array}{r} 400 \\ -\ 25 \\ \hline 375 \end{array}$$
; 375

4.
$$\begin{array}{r} 415 \\ +\ 98 \\ \hline 513 \end{array}$$
; 513

C. 1a. Elaine's Group
b. Max's Group
2a. 200
b. 500
3. C

D. 1. Judy's Recycling Box:

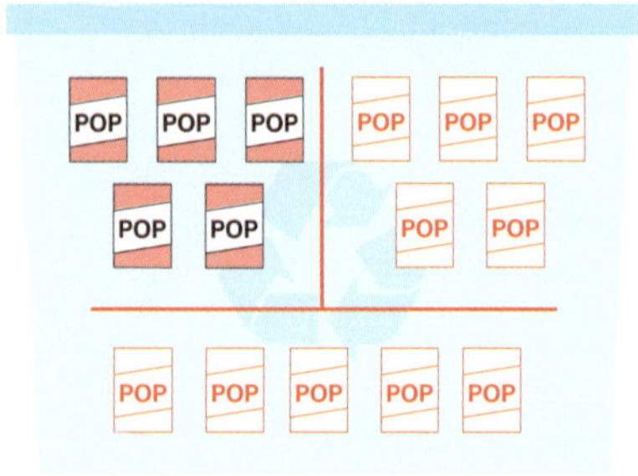

; 15

Leon's Recycling Box:

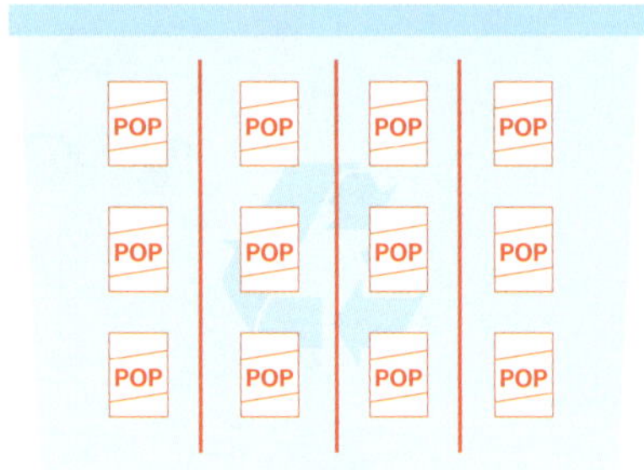

; 12

2. Judy's box
3. 185

Science

A. producers ; consumers

1.

2.

3.

B. (Trace the arrows.)
1. leaf ; beetle ; spider ; bird ; cat
2. clover ; grasshopper ; frog ; snake ; hawk
3. plankton ; water insect ; minnow ; largemouth bass ; osprey

ISBN: 978-1-77149-145-7

Social Studies

A.

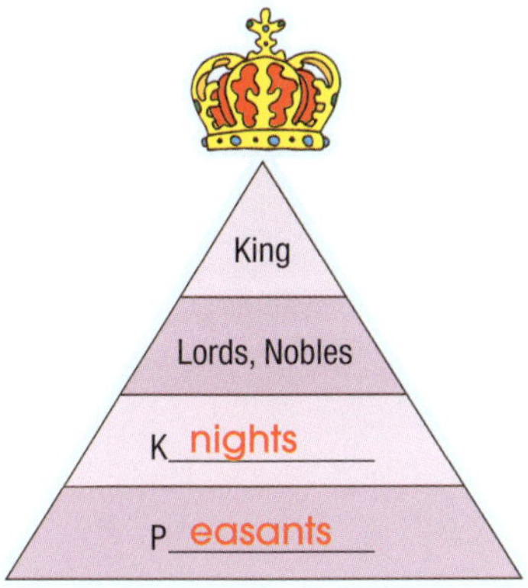

Knights: sons ; military
Peasants: protection ; land ; rent

B.

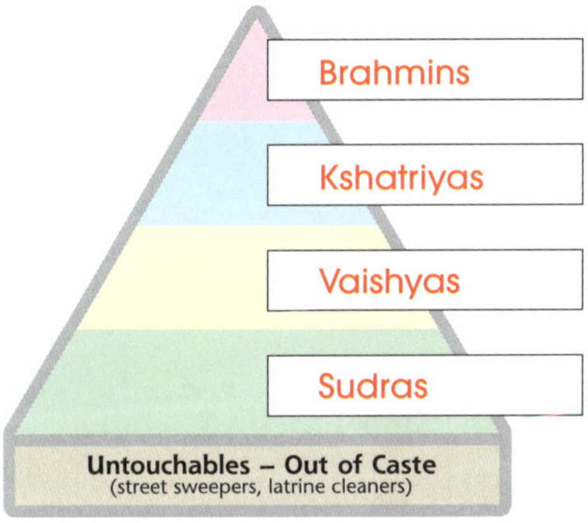

The untouchables were considered out of caste. They cleaned streets and latrines.

Week 2

English

A. 1. author
   2. orphanage
   3. "Mortimer"
   4. *Mud Puddle*

B. *Andrew's Loose Tooth* ; *Angela's Airplane* ; *Get Out of Bed* ; *I Have to Go* ; *Millicent and the Wind* ; *Mortimer* ; *Stephanie's Ponytail* ; *The Fire Station*

C. 1. Mud Puddle was Robert Munsch's first published book.
   2. Get Out of Bed is Peter's favourite book.
   3. Love You Forever became a bestseller in Canada.
   4. The Paper Bag Princess is a book about a brave girl who goes to rescue a prince from a dragon.

D.

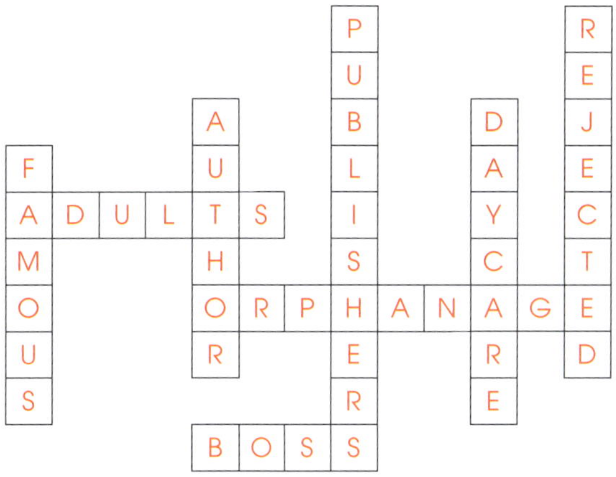

Mathematics

A. 5 cans ; 6 apples ; 9 cookies ; 4 cans

B. All-Purpose Flour: 2.62 ; 5.00 ; 2.38
   Baking Powder: 1.81 ; 2.00 ; 0.19
   Honey: 4.32 ; 10.00 ; 5.68
   Cream Cheese: 2.73 ; 3.00 ; 0.27

C.

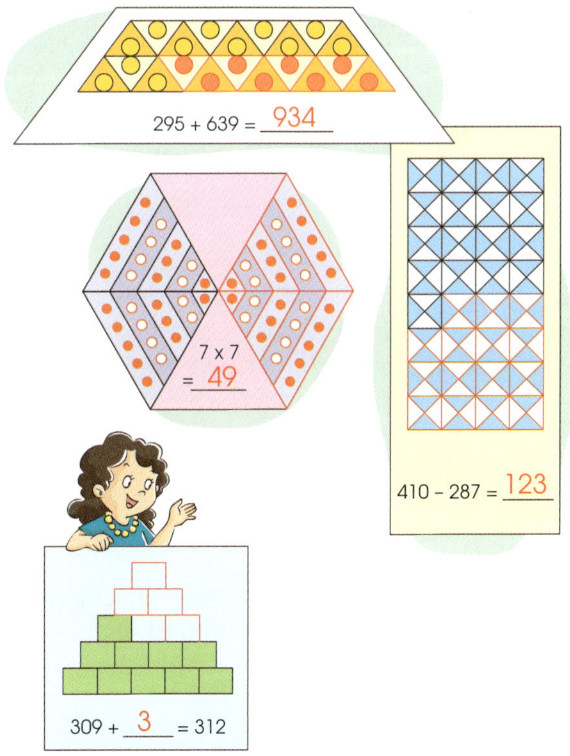

30 cm ; 34 cm ; 24 cm ; 24 cm

D. 220 ; 10
   200 ; 15
   190 ; 20
   180 ; 40
   160 ; 50

ISBN: 978-1-77149-145-7

Science

A.

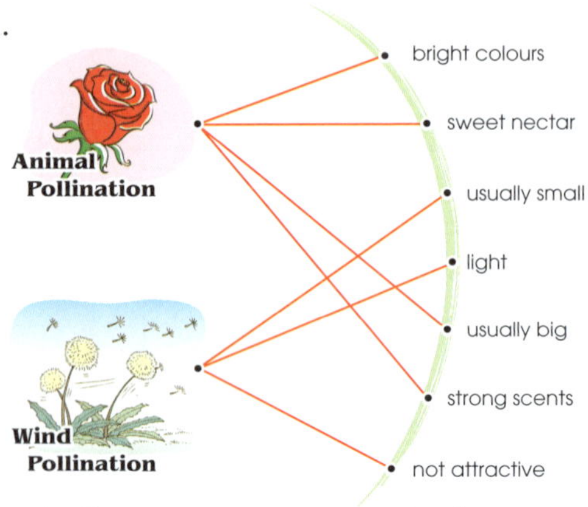

B. 1. B 2. A
3. E 4. D
5. C

Social Studies

A. land ; air ; water ; noise

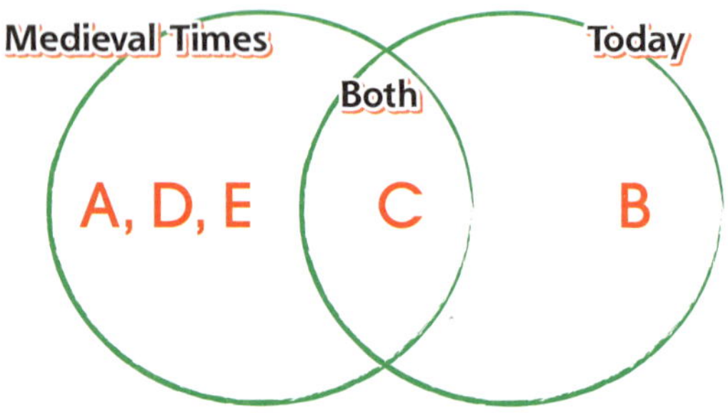

B. Past: ploughs or harrows drawn by oxen ; animal waste discharged into rivers
Present: ploughs or harrows drawn by tractors ; tractors and fertilizers

Week 3

English

B. Circle: movies ; batteries for flashlights ; popcorn ; hot dogs ; watermelon

C. (Individual answers)

D. (Suggested answers)
1. "I have a surprise for all of you," said Julia's mother.
2. Julia asked her mother, "Could we have pizza for dinner?"
3. "Let's make friendship bracelets for one another," suggested Julia.
4. "This is the best day ever," said Julia to her mother.

E. (Individual writing)

Mathematics

A.

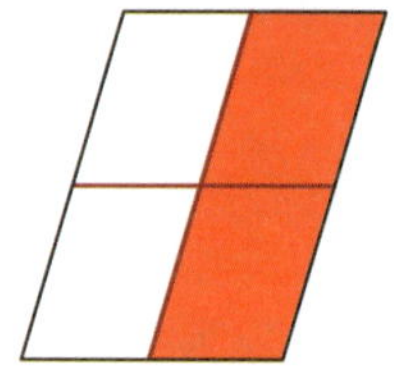
; $\frac{1}{2}$

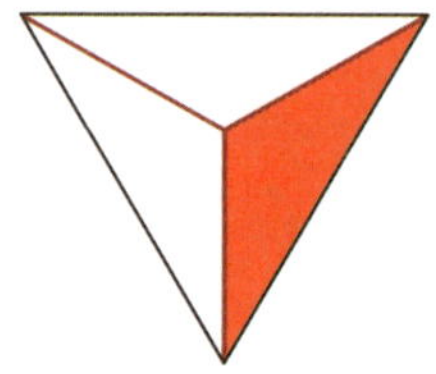
; $\frac{1}{3}$

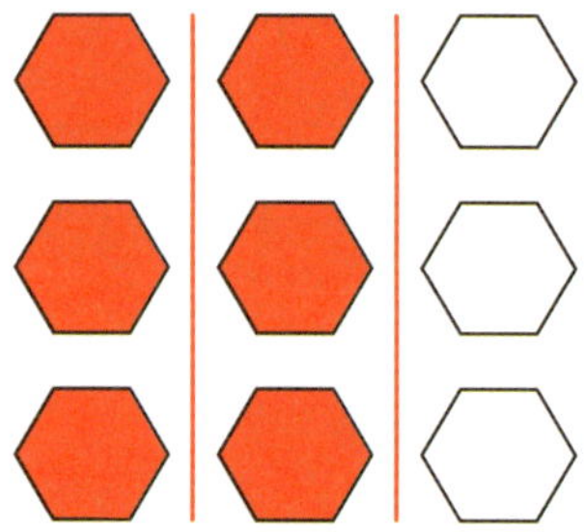
; $\frac{2}{3}$

; $\frac{3}{5}$

B. parallelogram ; 4 ; 4
triangle ; 3 sides ; 3 vertices
hexagon ; 6 sides ; 6 vertices
rhombus ; 4 sides ; 4 vertices

C.

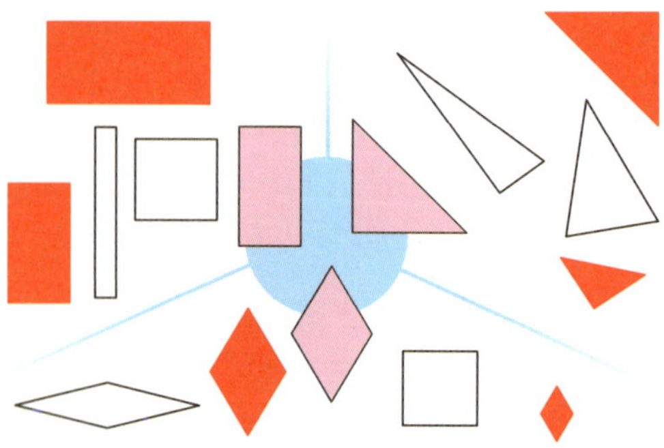

D. 1. Katie ; 90 marks
2. Ivy ; 50 marks
3. Ellen
4. 4 children

ISBN: 978-1-77149-145-7

E.

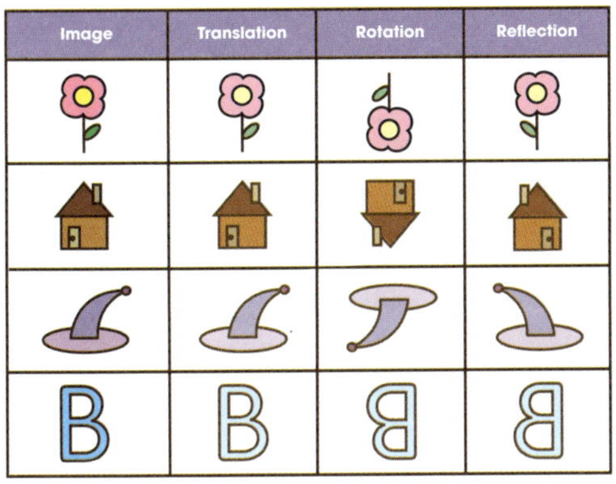

Science

A. 1a. unstable b. stable
2a. stable b. unstable
3. A: stable B: unstable
4a. stable b. unstable

B. 1. twist 2. squeeze
3. turn 4. bend
5. stretch 6. slide

Social Studies

A.

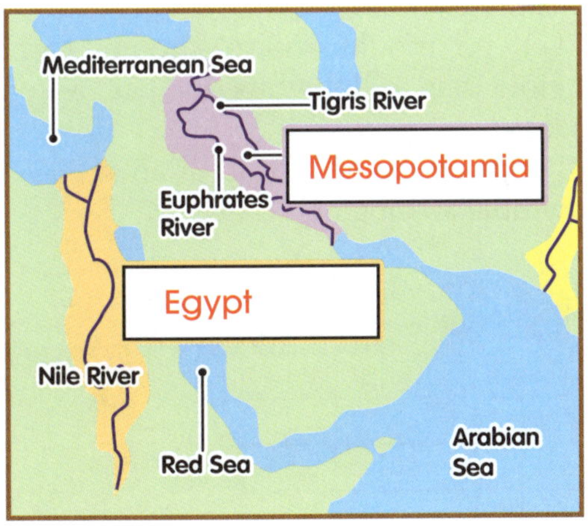

1. The settlements of both civilizations were around river areas.
2. (Suggested answer)
The rivers provided them with fresh water to drink.

B. 1. mud 2. wooden mould
3. mallet/copper chisel
4. copper chisel/mallet
5. wooden wedge
mud, wood, stones, rocks, and copper

Week 5

English

A. 1. Her mother said it was too dangerous.
2. She could not swim across the pool.
3. It is the tallest mountain in the world.
4. She went camping and stayed in a cottage on Pigeon Lake.
5. (Individual answer)

B. 1. vacation 2. miss
3. biking 4. created
5. coach 6. entire
7. tallest 8. dangerous

C. (Individual writing)

D. (Individual writing)

E. 1. I can't play street hockey this afternoon.
2. Maria couldn't find her sunglasses.
3. I've read stories about Mount Everest.
4. We're going camping in Algonquin Park.

F. (Individual writing and drawing)

Mathematics

A. (Suggested answers)

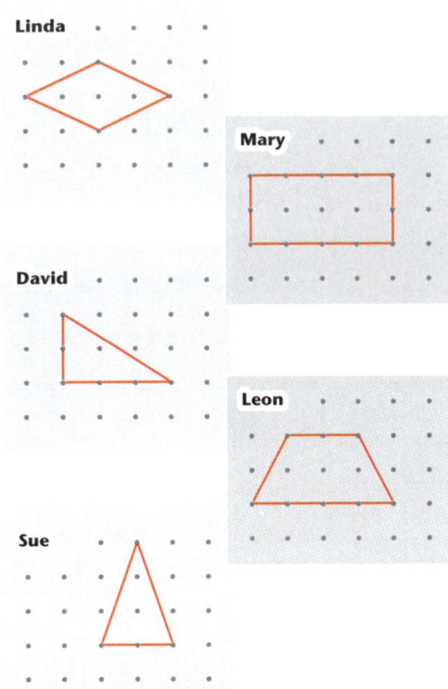

B. A: rectangular prism ; 6
B: triangular prism ; 5
C: rectangular pyramid ; 5
D: triangular pyramid ; 4
E: hexagonal prism ; 8
F: pentagonal pyramid ; 6

ISBN: 978-1-77149-145-7

C.

; 12

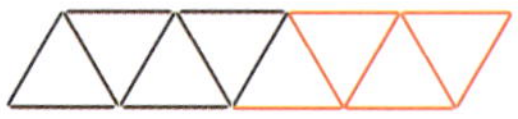

; 8

; 12

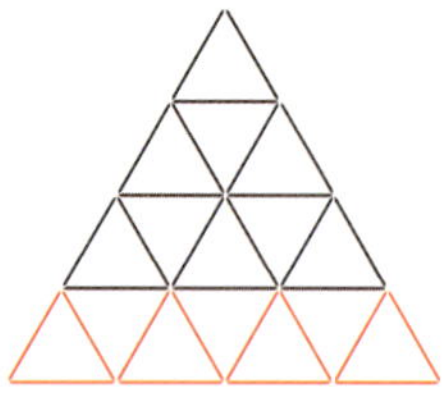

; 12

D. 80 + 2 ; 80 ; eighty
60 + 8 ; 70 ; seventy
40 + 7 ; 50 ; fifty
50 + 9 ; 60 ; sixty

Science

A. 1. bigger 2. cold
3. crack 4. soil
rocks ; small pieces ; soil

B. Humus ; decaying ; compost

t	k	e	g	g	s	h	e	l	l	s	g	w
e	w	h	v	e	g	e	t	a	b	l	e	s
a	b	v	q	a	d	s	f	t	w	n	v	l
b	l	s	o	i	l	y	g	l	f	u	l	e
a	c	n	c	z	f	r	u	i	t	g	j	a
g	r	a	s	s	s	m	v	w	m	r	p	v
s	z	v	j	z	p	l	a	n	t	s	k	e
c	o	f	f	e	e	g	r	o	u	n	d	s

Social Studies

A. water ;
plants ; otter ; turtle ; island ;
corn ;
good

B.

respect

Week 6

English

A. 1. It was a very bumpy ride, but it was worth it.
2. It was very easy to get lost in the old, enormous building.
3. A large, silver suit of armour at the end of a long corridor caught his attention.
4. (Suggested answer)
Larry felt his hand moving toward the doorknob.

B. 1. The teacher said, "The castle is very old and historic."
2. "Let's go into this room!" shouted Larry.
3. "How long will the bus ride be?" asked the class.
4. "I enjoyed the trip," said Brian.

C. (Individual writing and drawing)

D.

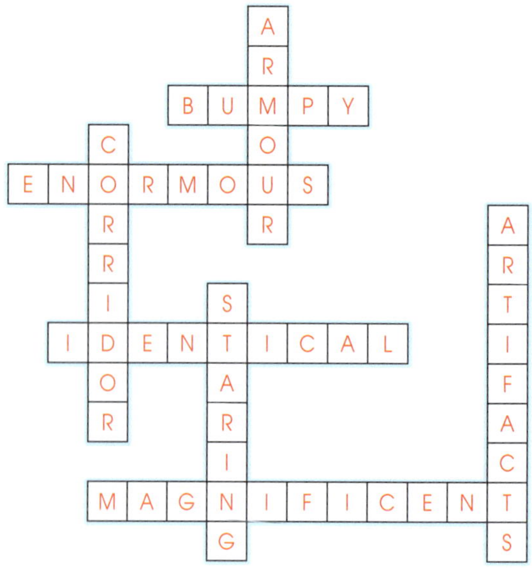

ISBN: 978-1-77149-145-7

Mathematics

A. 1. 4.60 ; 0.95 ; 1.09 ; 4.49 ; 3.60 ; 2.89
2. 5.69 ; 0.31
3. 5.44 ; 0.56
4. 10.09 ; 0.91

B. A:

30	99	**90**	63	22	**25**	**55**	**40**
10	43	**35**	108	49	68	84	**85**
20	**15**	**5**	**70**	457	**75**	**45**	**60**
32	72	**80**	503	9	**100**	752	37
356	102	**65**	6	207	**95**	**50**	**105**

761 ; 624 ; 42

B:

81	**24**	**30**	**42**	3
11	**2**	13	83	43
27	**10**	**6**	**28**	87
0	**14**	37	**44**	9
5	**38**	**26**	**50**	15

30 ; 14 ; 36

C:

32	**10**	**50**	**40**	42
13	25	22	**60**	8
34	**30**	**70**	**80**	93
62	**20**	36	31	72
36	**150**	**100**	**90**	39

615 ; 344 ; 717
A

C. 1. 4 ; 36
2. 36 ; $\frac{8}{36}$
3. 12 ; 36 ; $\frac{12}{36}$
4. 6
5. 18

D. 70 ; 65 ; 60
38 ; 36 ; 34
150 ; 175 ; 200
decrease ; 5
The numbers decrease by 2 each time.
The numbers increase by 25 each time.

Science

A. 1. rough 2. less 3. friction
4. more 5. force

B. 1a. grip b. slip
2a. grip b. slip
3a. grip b. slip
4a. slip b. grip

Social Studies

1. Ottawa
2. (Individual answer)
3. polar bears: Nunavut
grizzly bears: British Columbia
caribous: Newfoundland and Labrador
loons: Ontario
snowy owls: Quebec
deer: Saskatchewan
fish: Nova Scotia

Week 7

English

B. Cross out: a Cabbage Patch Kid doll, a drawing, a Care Bear

C.

													I
					U	N	U	S	U	A	L		N
									N				T
P				T	R	A	G	I	C				E
O									O				R
P									V				E
U									E				S
L					I	M	P	O	R	T	A	N	T
A									E				I
R	E	M	E	M	B	E	R	E	D				N
													G

D. (Individual answers)

E. (Individual writing)

F. 1. Dad planted trees in the backyard.
2. I needed a pen to write the letter.
3. My sister played in the sandbox.
4. We laughed at the dog's tricks.
5. I followed the path through the forest.

ISBN: 978-1-77149-145-7

G. drove ; dug ; wrote ; flew ; brought ; drank ; bought ; found

Mathematics

A. 1. impossible 2. possible
3. possible
4a. possible b. impossible
5. impossible

B. F ; T ; F ; T ; F ; T ; F ; T

C. 1.

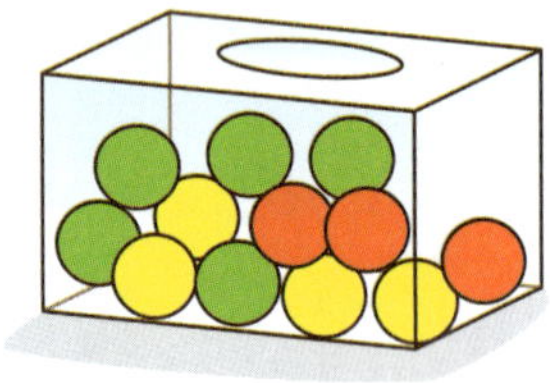

2a. Yes b. No
3a. a yellow ball
b. a green ball
4. (Suggested answers)
1st Combination:
Bag 1: 2
Bag 2: 3 ; 3
2nd Combination:
Bag 1: 1 green + 1 red
Bag 2: 4 green + 2 red

D. 1. Robot: 60 g House: 35 g
Soldier: 45 g Gift Box: 20 g
2. 135 g 3. 55 g
4.

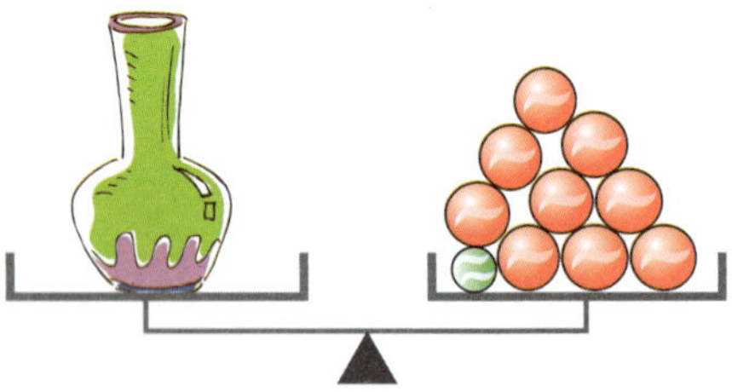

Science

A. Magnets ; magnetic ; iron ; two ; north ; south

B. 1. attracts 2. Unlike
3. repels 4. Like

5a.

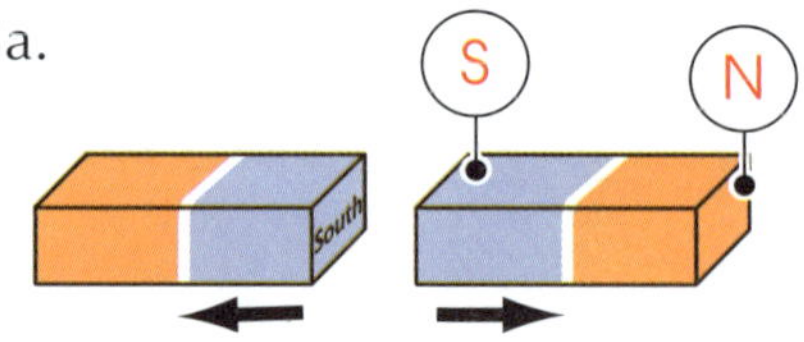

b.

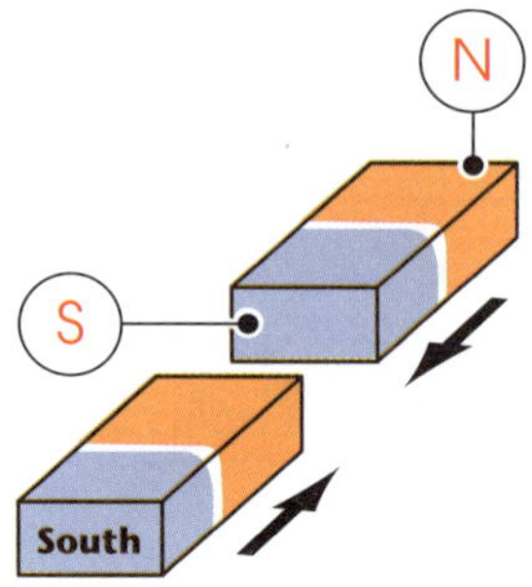

c.

Social Studies

A. Stage 1: natural forest
Stage 2: clear-cut area Stage 3: replantation

Stage 4: human-made forest

B. 1. Positive: It creates jobs.
Negative: Tourists can be careless and cause pollution.
2. (Individual answer)

ISBN: 978-1-77149-145-7